The Essential G...

Grow...
Orchids
in the Tropics

Chia Tet Fatt TEXT | David Astley PHOTOGRAPHY

mc **Marshall Cavendish**
Editions

© 2012 Marshall Cavendish International (Asia) Pte Ltd

Published in 2012; reprinted 2017

Published by Marshall Cavendish Editions
An imprint of Marshall Cavendish International

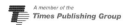
A member of the
Times Publishing Group

Other Marshall Cavendish Offices:
Marshall Cavendish Corporation. 99 White Plains Road, Tarrytown NY 10591-9001, USA • Marshall Cavendish International (Thailand) Co Ltd. 253 Asoke, 12th Flr, Sukhumvit 21 Road, Klongtoey Nua, Wattana, Bangkok 10110, Thailand • Marshall Cavendish (Malaysia) Sdn Bhd. Times Subang, Lot 46, Subang Hi-Tech Industrial Park, Batu Tiga, 40000 Shah Alam, Selangor Darul Ehsan, Malaysia

Marshall Cavendish is a registered trademark of Times Publishing Limited

National Library Board, Singapore Cataloguing-in-Publication Data

Chia, Tet Fatt, 1960-
The essential guide to growing orchids in the tropics / Chia Tet Fatt & David Astley. – Singapore : Marshall Cavendish Editions, c2011.
p. cm.
ISBN : 978-981-4351-39-3 (pbk.)
1. Orchid culture – Tropics. 2. Orchids – Tropics. I. Astley, David, 1948- II. Title.
SB409.5
635.93440913 – dc22   OCN748614194

Front cover: The flowers of a *Catasetum* hybrid (*Catasetum* Memoria Kampar Yip crossed with *Catasetum* Memoria Hon San). Orchids of the *Catasetum* genus, when grown in bright light, produce female flowers; grown in lower light, they produce male flowers. The male flowers seen on the cover are a striking burgundy red, and have an unusual trigger mechanism. When the two prominent white 'fangs' are touched by a pollinating insect, pollen shoots out and attaches to the unsuspecting creature.

Front flap: *Colmanara* Wildcat is a hardy, easy-to-grow hybrid that produces a long, arching inflorescence with 30–40 attractive flowers. There are many variants of Wildcat, most of which have yellow or dark-red flowers with brown markings. They like warm to cool conditions, semi-shade with good ventilation, and well-drained potting media.

Back cover: Close-up of *Miltonidium* Hawaiian Sunset (see page 27).

Back flap: Orchids make versatile decorative plants, taking to various potting media and growing conditions.

Page 1: The flower of the beautiful *Oncidium papilio* ('papilio' means butterfly) is carried one at a time on the inflorescence and is large and striking, often 10cm or more. It can be grown from the tropical lowlands up to the warm highlands.

Printed in Singapore by Fabulous Printers Pte Ltd

For orchid-lovers throughout the tropical world

CONTENTS

A *Cattleya* alliance hybrid with two showy flowers. The large, striking, red-purple frilled lip is typical of the *Cattleya* alliance hybrids and in this instance contrasts well with the creamy white flower. *Cattleya* orchids come from the New World of tropical and sub-tropical America.

PREFACE

The Essential Guide to Growing Orchids in the Tropics is different from other orchid books. Most books on tropical orchids have been written for specific regions of the tropics, or for people growing tropical orchids indoors or in greenhouses in cooler regions of the world.

This book has been written primarily for gardeners living in tropical countries – in any part of the world. That's not to say that orchid enthusiasts living in other regions won't find this book of interest – they will, because it will help them to understand how to replicate the natural growing environments for tropical orchids, which is a key factor in growing them successfully. But the primary intention of this book is to show gardeners in tropical countries how to grow healthy and free-flowering orchids – whether they live in the hot and humid tropical lowlands or the cool (and still humid!) tropical highlands. There's also advice for growing orchids in the desert regions of the tropics.

This book features photographs of many beautiful orchids from throughout the tropical world, and has been written to show, inspire and guide both beginners and orchid hobbyists on growing these fascinating plants.

Another difference with this book is that the photographs are of orchids from both the Old World (primarily Asia and tropical Australia) and the New World (the tropical Americas). While that means that not every plant photographed will be able to be grown outdoors in every region of the tropics, it provides the reader with an opportunity to appreciate the great diversity of orchid species that can be found in the tropics.

INTRODUCTION

One of the pleasures of tropical gardening is being able to grow plants with bright, colourful and unusual flowers throughout the year. There are many types of flowering plants that gardeners living in the tropics can choose to grow – but nothing beats tropical orchids for variety and exotic aura. These plants are hardy and easy to look after once their basic needs and requirements are understood.

Tropical orchids come in different forms, with flowers in a myriad of colours. In fact, the orchid family (known as Orchidaceae) is the largest family of plants in the flowering plant kingdom. There are currently over 25,000 orchid species and more than 125,000 orchid hybrids in the world – and tropical orchids constitute the vast majority. This means that tropical gardeners are spoilt for choice with a selection of more than 150,000 different types of orchids to grow. No other plant in the world comes close to the orchids in offering such a diverse selection.

History over the last few centuries has shown Man's obsession with orchids. These unusual tropical plants are able to grow on trees, and in the olden days, when modern science was still in its infancy, people in Europe thought they were parasites like mistletoes. Now it is known that they are not, and orchids simply use trees for anchorage, by wrapping their roots around the bark. Thus they are known as epiphytes. Though the majority of tropical orchids originate from jungles, where it is very humid, with plentiful rain throughout the year, they are at the same time great conservers of water. This is needed because by growing naturally on trees and rocks, the water supply is not consistent. Orchids conserve water in swollen modified stems called pseudobulbs and also in their thick and fleshy leaves.

The orchid plant architecture can be varied just like its flowers and there are infinite variations in body shapes and patterns. These unique and novel features of the plants, coupled with the fact that they come from steaming tropical jungles, drove Man's obsession with orchids into a frenzied state in the 19th century. Orchidophiles penned their experiences and encounters into stories that have been featured in novels, books and movies, many of which have become prized possessions as heirloom and collectors' items.

Indeed, orchids feature so highly in Man's outlook that until just 60 years ago, any household growing orchids was immediately considered wealthy. Though orchid

The national flower of Singapore since 1981, *Vanda* Miss Joaquim has been around for over a hundred years. In 1893 it became the first *Vanda* hybrid to be registered with the Royal Horticultural Society and has been widely grown throughout the tropics since.

A hybrid made in Thailand, *Dendrobium* Burana Royal x *Dendrobium* Green is a semi-standard green *Dendrobium* that has been used for an eye-catching display in the mist house of the Singapore National Orchid Garden – arguably the best orchid garden in the tropics.

prices have come down significantly due to technological advances in plant tissue culture (plant cloning), orchids to a certain extent are still considered a symbol of wealth and status in some societies even today. No other flowering plant is as heavily hybridised as orchids, which have a special worldwide registry and nomenclature for registration of new hybrids.

The word 'orchid' was coined over 2,000 years ago when it was adopted from the Greek word *orchis* – which means testicles. European orchids, which are mainly terrestrial, have swollen roots that look like the testicles of animals, and hence Europeans saw orchids as a representation of the male genitals. In the East, orchids have an equally long, if not longer, history. The ancient Chinese called orchids *lan*, which is associated with orchids whose flowers are fragrant. These fragrant Chinese orchids are mainly *Cymbidium ensifolia* and they were much admired in wealthy Chinese homes and are well-documented in ancient Chinese paintings.

The real treasure troves of tropical orchids were only discovered and collected 200 years ago when Europeans started to explore and colonise the world. They found the large-flowered *Cattleyas* from the tropical Americas, and the beautiful, long-lasting flowers of the *Vandas, Dendrobiums, Phalaenopsis* and *Paphiopedilums* of Asia, particularly Southeast Asia. Numerous massive orchid expeditions and collections were organised to these tropical jungles and many lives were lost. As well, many of the fine specimens collected from the jungles died during the shipment back to Europe and also in the trial-and-error period of learning how to grow tropical orchids in the temperate climate of Europe.

Growing the jungle orchids was much easier in the tropics: conditions were a lot more similar to the orchids' natural environment than were the greenhouses in Europe. Orchid growing was already very popular with the European colonisers in Southeast Asia way back in the 19th century. Many of the orchid species were grown in gardens, and it was noted that the species orchids flowered only seasonally, whereas the hybrid orchids were much more free-flowering. A good example is *Vanda* Miss Joaquim, a natural hybrid first discovered in 1893 in Singapore. Both its parents – *Vanda teres* from Myanmar and *Vanda hookeriana* from Perak, West Malaysia – flower infrequently in Singapore, while *Vanda* Miss Joaqium flowers freely throughout the year.

The beautiful flowers of this *Cattleya* alliance hybrid are the result of extensive breeding efforts by many different breeders over the years. The frilled fringes of the petals, especially the striking open lips, show that it is likely a trigeneric cross of *Brassavola, Laelia* and *Cattleya*; commonly called *Brassolaeliocattleya*, abbreviated as *Blc*. The hybrid loves partial sun and is easy to grow, flowering up to three times a year. Half a century ago, distinguished ladies of high social status would wear these flowers as a corsage with their outfits.

Careful hybridisation of orchids throughout the world over a century resulted in numerous beautiful and free-flowering orchids that are widely available in orchid nurseries today. Many multigeneric orchids have been bred with spectacular flowers and this is quite unlike any other plant. One reason for orchids being able to cross-hybridise across different genera is that orchids are relative young (50 million years) in terms of the evolutionary history of modern flowering plants (140 million years). As orchids are still actively evolving, they have the ability to interbreed across different genera. Also, orchid seeds are very small – like specks of dust – and each fruit capsule of an orchid may contain tens of thousands of seeds. The *Vanilla* orchid fruit capsule, for instance, can contain up to a million seeds. Orchids' seeds hold the record as the world's smallest. These characteristics allow for the breeding and selection of the numerous fine orchids we have today.

Vanilla fragrance comes from *Vanilla planifolia,* a climber from Mexico. Consequently this orchid has significant economic value. The greenish flower produces a large seed capsule that when ripe can be dried to produce the vanilla fragrance. It grows well in warm climates, but will only flower when the nights are cool.

Yes, the *Vanilla* orchid is where the ever-popular vanilla flavour comes from. The fragrance is derived from the seed pod. Many people don't realise that a flavour that is such a big part of modern-day culture and lifestyle, and used in

A live plant of the valuable *Dendrobium officinale* (Shi Hu) showing its healthy green canes before it is cut and dried. This plant is a little over 9 months old, and the longest elongating cane on the right (which is about 15 cm long) is 'ripe' enough to be harvested.

The cane of *Dendrobium officinale*, dried and curled into a tight ball, is sold in traditional Chinese medicine shops for improving lung function and alleviating backache problems. The highest-quality Shi Hu can cost up to US$10,000 per kg.

so many favourite foods – cakes, ice-cream, pastries and so on – comes from an orchid!

And it's not just in food flavouring that orchids make a contribution. There has been a surge of interest regarding the medicinal value of orchids that is spreading from Asia to all parts of the world. The tropical Chinese *Dendrobium* 'Shi Hu' is a prime mover in this area. It is used to attain brighter vision and treat backaches and for general well-being. The *Dendrobium* pseudobulbs are dried, twisted and curled into small compact balls; these are sold in traditional medicine shops from Japan to Singapore at high prices, with the best-quality ones fetching over US$10,000 per kg.

With such an exciting history, it is not surprising that orchids have a large worldwide appeal and following. Man's love for such exquisite plants can only be understood when time is spent growing and caring for the plants, and enjoying the reward of their beautiful flowers.

Tropical orchid growing is now 'big business' in most of the countries of Southeast Asia (especially Thailand and Singapore) and Central America (especially Costa Rica), northern Australia and Hawaii, where there are large wholesale nurseries producing both cut flowers and plants for the retail trade. In all of these regions and many other countries across the tropical world, there are many more smaller nurseries specialising in orchids for the home gardener.

In many countries, too, there are orchid societies bringing together enthusiasts who want to learn more about orchid growing and show their plants to others. These societies also provide an excellent opportunity to expand one's orchid collections through the exchanging of plants. Many such societies offer workshops on both basic and advanced propagation techniques and organise annual orchid shows for their members, so it is worthwhile becoming involved once interest has progressed beyond the beginner level.

Section 1 of this book assumes that the reader has no previous experience in growing orchids and provides a step-by-step guide to choosing, growing and caring for all types of tropical orchids in different regions of the tropical world. It explains in simple terms everything the beginner needs to know to successfully grow orchids for the first time – including a checklist of what to look for when buying orchids from a nursery or shop.

Section 2 of the book continues into the hobbyist's domain of propagating and repotting orchids, and discusses the special hygiene and nutritional needs of orchids. A large part of this section is devoted to the prevention of infection by diseases and attack by pests – major causes of orchid growers' frustration – and there is information on homemade recipes and remedies to combat diseases and pests for those gardeners who prefer non-toxic solutions.

Section 3 lists the most commonly grown tropical orchids with an easy-to-follow guide to the basic growing requirements for each genus.

Originating from the Philippines, *Grammatophyllum multiflorum* grows well in the hot tropical lowlands. The green flowers with brown markings are borne on an arching inflorescence of up to 1.5 metres in length, which may carry up to 100 flowers at a time.

Orchid Appreciation

No other group of plants has captured the imagination of Man like orchids. For hundreds of years collectors have risked their lives exploring the jungles of the world looking for new species. Many say that orchids are the most beautiful and alluring plants in the world. Some collectors admit to being obsessed with orchids. What is it that makes these exotic plants so special?

Orchids are different from other plants in that they can be admired from the apex of their inflorescence right down to the tip of their roots. Take *Vanda* orchids as an example: the flowers are gorgeous and they come in a myriad of colours – and they are long-lasting too! Some are sweetly scented, like *Vanda* Mimi Palmer. The stiff leaves of the *Vanda* are arranged in two distinct rows, giving some plants an orderly 'architectural' look.

Vandas are much sought after for aesthetic flower arrangements and displays in 5-star hotels because their roots can form part of the arrangement too. Just growing a *Vanda* in an empty hanging basket will allow the roots to hang freely in the air, giving an exotic and aesthetic display of beautiful silver roots with fresh green root-tips – a sight that is pleasing to both the eyes and the mind.

Vanda is just one genus. The hundreds of other genera and thousands of other species include plants that are unique in their own special ways. This is the essence of the beauty of orchids – no other plants in the world have such variety of form, colour and individual appeal.

The massive flower of a very healthy *Phragmipedium kovachii* plant. This is a much sought-after species, having been discovered only in 2001 in Peru; the first plant offered for sale in 2002 was rumoured to cost US$10,000. Since then it has been heavily hybridised as it is the largest flower in the *Phragmipedium* genus. The flower can grow to 20 cm across.

Commonly called the Bottlebrush Orchid, *Dendrobium smilliae* has pinkish-white flowers with a shiny green lip in an eye-catching compact inflorescence. It is easy to grow and, coming from Papua New Guinea and northern Australia, tolerates warm to hot conditions.

An impressive mass of bright-pink *Phalaenopsis* flowers. These hybrid *Phalaenopsis* flowers are long-lasting (up to 3 months), and are commonly known as moth orchids. They love the shade and are great for beginners to grow.

01

GROWING ORCHIDS
FOR BEGINNERS

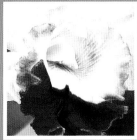

ORCHID SPECIES AND HYBRIDS

All orchid *species* are the products of natural selection (i.e. untouched by Man). As such, most of them are well-attuned to the specific environment in which they are naturally found. When Man collects and grows them, the environmental intricacies needed for successful growth may not be reproducible away from the wild, and therefore they may not flower. In the wild, many orchids are seasonal in flowering, and a large number only flower occasionally. For this reason, unless a particular species of orchid is known to be free-flowering, it is best for beginners to choose hybrid plants, otherwise they may end up growing only the plants.

Hybrids, in contrast to species, are the offspring of Man cross-pollinating different genera or species of orchids.

This popular *Cattleya* hybrid is loved the world over, and the specimen in the picture is the unifoliate single-flowered variety that can easily grow to over 10 cm in diameter. Light purple is a 'standard' colour in *Cattleya* hybrids. The lip is always the most outstanding feature of these plants.

Most hybridisation is undertaken to produce more spectacular flowers or to combine the best traits of different orchids. Extensive hybridisation over the past 50 years – through careful selection of the most desirable traits – has improved tremendously the orchid flower form, its spectrum of colours, and its free-flowering properties.

There are more than five times as many registered orchid hybrids than there are species orchids (and many more that are not registered). Generally speaking, it is easier to grow orchid hybrids than species. Hybrids are usually

This hybrid called *Beallara* Pacific Pastel 'Massive' is the product of a complex crossing of four genera (*Brassia, Cochlioda, Miltonia and Odontoglossum*) and is therefore given a new status in genera known as *Beallara*. It is easy to bloom and produces large, white flowers with pastel-red to maroon patterns. The plant can grow quite large, with prominent pseudobulbs, and makes a great show plant. It needs cooler temperatures to flower, hence it is best suited to the tropical highlands; that said, this one was photographed growing near sea level in Hawaii.

more vigorous and free-flowering than the species parents – due to the increase of alleles (variation of a gene) resulting in a more robust genome. However, there is an important caveat, and that is as the hybrid complexity increases, the vigour of the plant may decrease. This is because over-hybridisation of the plants can destabilise the genome and gene expression. That is the science of it; the practical rule is to buy free-flowering *primary* hybrids.

How orchids are named

The naming of orchids follows what is known as the 'scientific binomial classification system', where the name of each orchid has two parts, for example *Vanda teres*, where *Vanda* is the genus and *teres* is the species. There are many types of *Vanda* orchids, but only one *Vanda teres* species. As *teres* is a natural species, the species name is not capitalised. When orchid names are written in text, both the genus and species are italicised. If that is not possible for some reason, then they are underlined instead.

When *Vanda teres* was crossed with *Vanda hookeriana*, a new Vanda hybrid was produced, and it was registered and named *Vanda* Miss Joaquim. As 'Miss Joaquim' is not a natural species, it is not italicised, and the name is capitalised.

When the names of two orchids being crossed to produce a hybrid are written – for example: *Vanda teres* x *Vanda hookeriana* – the plant producing the seed pod is written before the plant producing the pollen. Hence *teres* is the pod plant and *hookeriana* is the pollen plant.

An attractive showy lip in red and white forms the highlight of *Miltonidium* Hawaiian Sunset – an intergeneric hybrid between *Miltonia* and *Oncidium*. It is vigorous in growth and produces a long spike of inflorescence with many flowers which are slightly fragrant.

The extensive breeding efforts in *Cattleya* have led to numerous hybrids of good-quality flowers. This 'Green Emerald', its spotted sepals and petals contrasting well with the bright pink lip, is testimony to successful breeding.

History of hybridisation

The first man-made orchid hybrid, *Calanthe Dominyi* (*Calanthe furcata* x *Calanthe masuca*), was crossed in 1853 and flowered in 1856. To date more than 125,000 orchid hybrids have been made from the 25,000 or so orchid species discovered by Man. This is because orchids hybridise easily not only within the same genus but across similar genera as well.

Hybrids are fertile and can be used for further crossings. As such, many of the hybrids today are not primary hybrids, but secondary hybrids and beyond. Although it is more than 150 years since the first crossing, new hybrids are still constantly being produced in the orchid world. Orchid hybrids can be registered with the Royal Horticulture Society at Kew Gardens in London, which approves the name after checking with its records of all the other registered hybrids in the International Orchid Register.

Nobody knows how many unregistered hybrids there are, but it is likely to be many thousands because some commercial growers don't register their hybrids in order to keep the parentage of their plants secret.

This recently introduced hybrid of *Paphiopedilum insigne* parentage had a retail price of US$400 – not unusual for newly introduced hybrids and varieties. Many orchids can be purchased for just a few dollars, but the rarer and more sought-after plants can make orchid growing an expensive hobby for serious collectors. All green flowers of the slipper orchid are based on albino flowers that are unable to produce anthocyanin pigments and can be traced to *Paphiopedilum insigne*. This species comes in green and various shades of yellowish green.

An interesting hybrid, this *Phalaenopsis* is the product of *P. lobbii* x *P. tetrapis*. Though the purplish-red petals of *P. tetrapis* (from the mangrove forests of Sumatra) are missing, the dominant yellow lip of *P. lobbii* (from the Himalayas) is still very distinctive in this progeny.

A *Mokara* hybrid with an evenly toned bright yellow inflorescence. This is a worthwhile trait in orchids because in many yellow flowers, the older ones fade with time, leading to uneven tone. The genus *Mokara* is a product of a trigeneric parentage of *Arachnis*, *Vanda* and *Ascocentrum*.

The distinctive bright-red flowers of these *Renanthera* hybrids are borne on a large inflorescence. They are sun-loving but will still grow well in light shade. Like many hybrid orchids, they flower freely throughout the year.

The rich yellow flowers of the *Oncidium* Moon Shadow, with their yellow and dark-chocolate edges, stand out strikingly against the green leaves. They last over a month, and the plant is easy to maintain.

BASIC ORCHID ANATOMY AND GROWTH HABITS

In order to grow orchids successfully, it is necessary to know a little about their anatomy and their growth habits. Orchidaceae is the largest plant family in the world, comprising about 25,000 species of orchids and over 125,000 hybrids. Their growth habits are extremely varied. Orchids grow on trees, on rocks and in the ground, in diverse habitats ranging from the tropics to the sub-polar regions, and from sea level into the high mountains.

Despite this variability, orchids usually display one of two forms of growth: monopodial or sympodial. Monopodial orchids grow along one axis; sympodial orchids grow along two.

MONOPODIAL ORCHIDS

For monopodial orchids, growth takes place along a single axis: upwards. As it grows, the stem of the monopodial orchid forms new leaves along the way. This makes them climbing orchids (with the exception of some compact forms). A good example of a monopodial orchid is the well-known *Vanda*, which grows taller and taller with time. The growth of monopodial orchids is indeterminate, and as the tip of the stem continues growing upwards, flowering takes place from axillary buds all along the stem.

There are three forms of monopodial orchids: compact, intermediate and long-stemmed. The *Phalaenopsis* orchid

A *Phalaenopsis* hybrid, commonly known as the Moth Orchid, is a compact monopodial. The flowers are long-lasting – up to three months if well cared for – and the red striation and spots beautifully accentuate the flower.

belongs to the compact short-stemmed form. Even with age it does not grow tall – at most 30 cm in height. The *Vanda* orchid, on the other hand, is more of an intermediate type, and will grow to 60–90 cm in time. The really lengthy monopodials grow very quickly and ramble to over two metres within two years. Good examples include *Arachnis* and *Vanilla*.

As most monopodial orchids are climbers, it means that as they grow, they produce roots from the stem. These aerial roots are normally thick and sturdy, and attach themselves firmly to any structure (wood or metal) with which they come into contact. Over time, this root system becomes highly extensive. Side-shoots may also form at the basal portion of the plant as they get older; these can be detached and propagated once they produce three roots.

A monopodial orchid, *Vanda* Mimi Palmer has a strong, pleasant fragrance that makes it popular with growers. It is very free-flowering under medium light, each inflorescence producing about 10–12 flowers.

Trichoglottis philippinensis has a characteristic long climbing stem, with leaves arranged in an ever-orderly zig-zag pattern. This trait is also seen in the inflorescence arrangement. The flowers come in many shades from maroon-red to the brownish colour seen in the photograph. It grows well in bright indirect light and looks stunning when the flowers bloom en masse. Make sure that the pot does not dry out completely.

SYMPODIAL ORCHIDS

The majority of tropical orchids are sympodial. A sympodial orchid grows in two directions: horizontally and vertically. Growth along the horizontal axis is indeterminate. This means that the plant grows by creeping slowly across the pot, from one side to the other. The secondary growth, however, is often more apparent to the eyes, and this is the growth of the pseudobulbs (swollen modified stems), which is determinate. The stems of sympodial orchids are not highly visible, unlike the pseudobulbs which normally grow as a cluster from the base of the previous pseudobulb.

The flowers of sympodial orchids can originate from different locations of the plant – usually the tip of the pseudobulb or along its length or from its base, but also from the rhizome-like stem. The roots, though, are always at the base of the pseudobulb and/or along the rhizome-like stem.

Common examples of sympodial orchids are *Dendrobium, Oncidium* and *Cattleya*. With *Dendrobium* orchids, the pseudobulb is in the form of a thick fleshy cane that bears up to a dozen leaves and will flower only after the pseudobulb stops growing. Flowering starts at the apex and continues downwards along the cane – in contrast to monopodial orchids. *Oncidium* orchids have rather short, fleshy pseudobulbs, and inflorescence is borne from the base of the pseudobulb. With *Cattleya* orchids, the pseudobulbs are similarly short and fleshy, but inflorescence is borne instead from the apex of the one- or two-leaf pseudobulb.

A young potted *Dendrobium* Golden Blossom showing the distinctive thick and juicy pseudobulbs. They function as a very important storage organ in orchids. Fresh and healthy pseudobulbs should not be trimmed as new growths depend on them for water and nutrients during their rapidly growing phase. Pseudobulbs in *Dendrobium* orchids are also the source for the new inflorescence. Note the variegated yellow leaf margin of this particular hybrid – an additional feature that enhances the plant's beauty.

The yellow flowers of *Dendrobium* Golden Blossom, with their eye-catching dark brown lips, are indeed showy. This hybrid, whose parents are from northern Thailand, is seasonal in flowering.

Cattleya Hailstorm is a popular multiflora *Cattleya* with 5–8 flowers per inflorescence. It is a primary hybrid (*C. bowringiana* x *C. skinneri*) and the purple colour is typical of the *Cattleya* genus. This specimen shows its capability for mass flowering, which gives a stunning display.

The sympodial *Cattleya aclandiae* is much used in *Cattleya* breeding. Its dominant traits – the brown spots in the sepals and petals, as well as the striking lip – are very dominant, and can be traced in the many present-day hybrids that are its progeny.

PARTS OF THE ORCHID

Like any normal plant, the orchid consists of roots, stem, leaves and inflorescence. As most tropical orchids are epiphytic (meaning they grow on trees, rather than in the ground), they possess thick fleshy leaves and pseudobulbs that enable them to conserve water. These leaves and pseudobulbs fix carbon dioxide at night, which is stored as malic acid and used for photosynthesis during the day.

Healthy *Vanda* roots exhibit bright jade-green root tips and clean, white velamen covering the rest of the root surface. Strong and actively growing roots that are able to attach themselves firmly onto the substrate bark are a good indicator of the healthy state of these plants.

ORCHID ROOTS

Orchids have most intriguing roots. They are either aerial or terrestrial. One thing that marks an orchid root is the velamen layer. This silvery-white layer – the outermost layer of the root – is spongy and has lots of cellular air spaces that absorb and retain water. Aerial roots normally

These orchids growing out of hanging clay pots in Thailand are *Vandas*, commonly-grown epiphytes in the tropical lowlands. They have thick storage roots and are perfect for hanging in pots or baskets without any potting media – the clay pots are actually empty! The numerous roots, which appear to 'flow' downwards, are important for the growth and flowering of the plant and should not be cut unless they are dried up and dead. These plants need watering once or twice a day.

This *Vanda coerulea* hybrid is just growing hanging from a wire attached to the roof of a shed without any pot or media and yet it flowers beautifully. If it can grow like this, what is the point of having a pot or basket? *Vanda coerulea* and its hybrids are capable of growing 'in the air' in partial sunlight when they are properly watered daily in high humidity and with gentle ventilation.

have green root tips, which are photosynthetic, meaning that they can fix sugar compounds using sunlight. When these aerial roots touch a surface such as the bark of a tree or a rock, they secrete a glue-like substance which helps them adhere firmly to the surface of these objects, thus anchoring the orchid plant in place. When an orchid plant is healthy, its roots can grow very quickly to several metres.

The roots at the base of some epiphytic/terrestrial orchids, such as the *Grammatophyllum* species, are very interesting. They come in two forms: thick, burrowing substrate roots, and fine but leathery upward-pointing aerial roots. These latter form a pot-like structure that, in the plant's natural habitat, efficiently capture falling leaf litter. The captured leaves gradually decompose within the matted mass of roots, becoming organic fertiliser for the plant.

The tender root tips of this *Phalaenopsis* orchid have been eaten by pests – possibly snails, cockroaches or even mice. The root on the extreme left is clearly dying as the velamen is turning brown.

ORCHID LEAVES

Orchid leaves come in various shapes and sizes, but are all what botanists classify as 'simple' leaves. Some orchids' leaves are quite unusual, such as those of the *Paraphalaenopsis* and terete *Vanda*, which are cylindrical. Others can be V-shaped, with the strap-leaf *Vanda* being a good example. Most orchid leaves are thick, leathery or succulent. These features tell us that the leaves function as storage organs for water and food. Most orchids' leaves last a long time on the plant, but for some orchids, they shed their leaves annually, especially during dry periods, and go into a period of dormancy.

Variegation is a trait much sought after by many orchid enthusiasts. It can be obtained through mutations in tissue culture or through the use of chemical mutagens. The large band of variegation in the leaves of this *Phalaenopsis amabilis* gives added colour to the plant.

The fish-bone formation of this *Vanda* hybrid's semi-terete leaves gives the plant a remarkable presence. This healthy specimen, mounted on a tree, is doing very well, as can be seen from the vibrant red flowers, strong roots and bright green leaves. Daily watering is required to prevent it from drying out.

With their light-green mottling, the tessellated leaves of *Paphiopedilum bellatulum* are especially attractive. The solitary large whitish-cream flower with reddish-brown spots has a definitive shape that makes the plant a collector's item. The flowering period is in spring and it is long-lasting. In its native habitats in Myanmar, Thailand and southern China, it is found in limestone hills growing in crevices filled with leaf mold; in cultivation it grows best in diffuse light, in humus-rich potting mix with some limestone added.

Best known for its large, slightly green flower with fimbriated lips, *Rhyncholaelia digbyana* is responsible for the large frilly lips on most of today's modern *Cattleya* hybrids. It exudes an alluring fragrance in the evening. The plant has sturdy, stiff, upright light-green leaves that when grown in strong light turn reddish-purple. It does best in the cooler regions of the tropics, near the sub-tropics, and requires plenty of ventilation.

ORCHID FLOWERS

The basic pattern of the orchid flower is 3+3, which means three sepals and three petals. In most orchids, the sepals are very colourful and showy, just like petals. (Some people thus group the sepals and petals of the orchid flower as one and call them tepals.) By far the most characteristic trait of the orchid flower, however, is the conversion of the third petal into a lip. This lip serves as the landing pad for the insect pollinator and can come in very diverse shapes, sizes and colours.

The tepals are all attached between the base of the column and above the ovary. The column is actually a fusion of the female and male organs of the flower: the stigma is found on the ventral (bottom) side of the column, while the pollen is found below the anther cap.

This *Spathoglottis* flower clearly shows the 3+3 (three sepals and three petals) layout that is typical of all orchid blooms, with the third petal converted into a showy lip. The flower is very likely a hybrid between a purple *Spathoglottis plicata* with a yellow *Spathoglottis kimbaliana*. It is a sun-loving terrestrial orchid and will bloom throughout the year, perfect for beds and pots. It requires a free-draining soil or potting mix with plenty of organic matter incorporated.

Orchid pollen is unlike the powdery pollen of flowers like the rose. In orchids, the pollen is packed tightly together in two or more distinct masses called pollinia. These sticky pollinia become attached to the insect pollinator and are thus transferred to the stigma of another flower. It is interesting to note that the first flower to go into space was an orchid, and one of the reasons was precisely that orchid pollen, being in a tied mass, is not air-dispersed like other flowers', and hence would not damage the spacecraft's electronic instruments or trigger hay fever in the astronauts.

The fantastic appearance of *Zygopetalum* Lois comes from the dramatic contrast between the tepals (sepals that look like petals) and the lip. This genus produces many plants that are much sought after by orchid collectors. It is a cool-loving species with an ancestry in the mountains of Brazil.

The bright yellow pollinia is just visible beneath the translucent anther cap of this *Phalaenopsis amabilis*. The striking lip shows colourful yellow and red markings, most intense on the callus hump. The lip tapers at the end into two elongated flagella.

A semi-terete *Vanda* orchid with its anther cap removed to show the bright yellow pollinia. A single fruit capsule can contain hundreds of thousands of tiny seeds.

Pollinia from a *Phalaenopsis* orchid (left) and a *Vanda* orchid (right), with the tip of a ballpoint pen providing scale. The bi-lobed pollinia is attached by a clear membrane with a sticky pad at the bottom that adheres to the insect pollinator, by which it gets carried to another flower where pollination occurs.

Pollinia of different orchids (from left to right): *Vanda*, *Cattleya* and *Phalaenopsis*. Sympodial orchids like *Cattleya* have pollinia that are separate (in this photograph they are still attached to the anther cap), while the pollinia of monopodial orchids like *Vanda* and *Phalaenopsis* are joined.

The yellow pollinia of a *Brassolaeliocattleya* flower is found behind the anther cap. All orchids' pollinia, when matured, are either bright yellow or orange.

The colourful frilly lip of *Brasso-laeliocattleya* Hawaiian Wizard 'Volcano Queen' stands out vividly from the whitish-pink flowers. This plant is grown with the right amount of filtered light, as can be seen from the light-green leaves.

The *Dracula* orchid is a young genus created only in 1978 from the *Masdevallia* genus, which is why it has the long tepals that taper to a pointed end – similar to the *Masdevallia*. They come from higher elevation cloud forests in the tropical Americas, and thus require cool to cold growing conditions.

The pink flower of *Lycaste* Macro Devosiana displays a characteristic feature of the genus: the inner petals being much reduced compared to the larger sepals. This plant is flowering after a dormant period when the leaves have dropped and the swollen pseudobulbs have rested.

The extended yellow flower spike of this *Stelis immersa* looks as if it grew out from the middle of the leaf. Note that the third oldest flower was pollinated and is developing into a green fruit capsule. The plant is epiphytic and can be grown on tree bark and in pots. This genus generally has inconspicuous flowers and therefore tends to be grown by orchid collectors specialising in miniature orchids, rather than gardeners looking for showy flowers. It can be found growing in highland regions from Mexico down to Venezuela.

This *Dendrobium* King Dragon hybrid is rather unusual, because of its peloric flowers with different shades of colour. In peloric flowers, the petals become lip-like.

The unifoliate *Brassolaeliocattleya* hybrid produces two large yellow flowers with red frilly lips. Note that the petals show a slight peloric mutation, i.e. are slightly lip-like, with the red lip pigmentation. This warm-loving plant is easy to cultivate in lowland regions.

GROWTH HABITS OF ORCHIDS

EPIPHYTES, LITHOPHYTES AND TERRESTRIALS

Orchids are also categorised according to the medium in or on which they grow.

If they are growing on trees (normally on the tree trunk or branches), they are termed epiphytic. They acquire nutrients and water from the run-offs from the bark and branches rather than from the tree itself, so they are not considered parasitic. A large majority of tropical orchids are epiphytes, including popular genera such as *Phalaenopsis, Dendrobium* and *Oncidium.*

Epiphytic orchids grow on trees. This unique property can be capitalised on for landscaping tropical gardens, to give them an exotic ambience.

A clump of orchids of the *Cattleya* alliance growing on rock. Note the rambling network of healthy roots, especially those that are thicker and whitish in colour, which are covering the rock surface. This lithophytic capability is present in many epiphytic orchid species.

Epiphytic orchids such as *Oncidium stenotis* can be grown mounted on wood. This grower has done a secondary mounting by placing the piece of wood with the orchid plant onto the trunk of a palm tree. This is not ideal, however, as the weight of the extra piece of wood puts stress on the orchid root growth. A better way is to mount the orchids directly onto the tree, with moisture-absorbent material (such as sphagnum moss or coconut fibre) behind the orchid plant, and tie them firmly with plastic-coated wire, strong garden twine or raffia tape.

Lithophytic orchids theoretically grow on the surfaces of rocks and boulders; they include members of the *Eria* and *Epidendrum* genera. In reality, however, many lithophytic orchids also grow on trees, and conversely, many epiphytic orchids grow on rocks. That is why a large majority of the *Dendrobium* and *Vanda* tribes take equally well to wood bark, charcoal, broken bricks or lava rocks.

Terrestrial orchids are ground-dwelling; they like well-drained soil with a top layer of rich organic matter. Common ones in this category from Southeast Asia are *Arundina, Paphiopedilum* and *Spathoglottis*. Other examples include *Disa* from Africa, and *Dracula* from tropical America. Unlike epiphytic and lithophytic orchids, which can normally cross-over in their growth habitat, terrestrial orchids are rather rigid in their growing medium requirements. Hence, it is necessary to know what these requirements are to achieve good growth.

The highly adaptable *Rhynchostele bictoniense* has been found in its native highland habitats across Central America growing on trees (epiphytic), on rocks (lithophytic) and in the ground (terrestrial). The tall inflorescence always grows from a newly formed pseudobulb.

A terrestrial orchid by definition, *Paphiopedilum spicerianum* is sometimes also found growing as a lithophyte. It is a distinctive species of the *Paphiopedilum* genus, with its large white dorsal sepal arching over the lip like the operculum of a pitcher plant. It comes from northeastern India, Bhutan, northern Myanmar and China's Yunnan province. First seen in Europe in 1878, it was named after a collector, a Mr Herbert Spicer, who later sold the orchid for 75 guineas – a large sum of money in those days.

The long-caned *Dendrobium fimbriatum* is not too fussy about where it grows – it has been found growing as an epiphyte, lithophyte and terrestrially in the highlands of northern Thailand where it originates. Although it has rather messy growth habits, it is easy to grow in large gardens in cooler highland localities; it produces arching canes up to two metres long, with an inflorescence of bright yellow flowers with an eye-catching black-based lip. It grows well attached to a tree, where it will receive dappled sunlight throughout the day.

Commonly known as the jewel orchid because of its bright and attractive leaf venations, the shade-loving *Ludisia discolor* is strictly terrestrial and grown for its foliage. The small white flowers are not attractive. It needs to be grown in rich soil with high organic content.

GROWING MEDIA

Dendrobium jenkinsii (also known as *Den. aggregatum var jenkinsii*) is a deciduous miniature orchid that produces bright orange-yellow flowers that are very attractive. This plant is well established on an old tree branch but would probably do even better if it was on tree fern bark or cork, which holds a little more moisture. *Dendrobium jenkinsii* will develop into quite a large specimen, so a good-size mount should be provided at the start so that there is as little disturbance as possible later on. It should not be fertilised in the cooler months.

Trees and rock faces provide 'natural' places to grow epiphytic and lithophytic orchids, but not every gardener has suitable trees and very few have natural rock faces in their gardens. It is for this reason that most orchids are grown in pots.

The selection of growing media for pot-grown orchids is very important in the tropics. In the lowland wet tropics, the golden rule is to select growing media that will not decompose rapidly under the high temperatures and rainfall that are typical of most tropical lowland climates. Many potting mixes that are suitable for growing orchids

in temperate climates are not suitable for these regions at all. Examples are wood chips and sphagnum moss. Under cool greenhouse conditions where temperature and watering are controlled, orchids may grow well in such media, but if grown in the tropics outdoors, the heat and rain cause rapid decay. This in turn adversely affects root growth, often leading to death of the roots.

Orchid growers in the tropics have tried and tested various potting media using local materials. For example, for more than 80 years, growers in Southeast Asia and northern Australia have used a 1:1 mix of charcoal (from mangroves) and broken bricks. With this mix, in clay pots

Macadamia nut shells are used as growing medium for *Dendrobium* orchids at a Costa Rica orchid cut-flowers farm. In this instance the plants seem to be doing well, albeit a little on the skinny side, perhaps due to insufficient fertiliser and watering. The fallen leaves and dried inflorescence amongst the shells should be removed to improve farm hygiene.

The whitish substrate used as potting media in these nursery pots is pumice. *Ansellia africana* is dainty epiphytic orchid with striking lips, originating from the African continent. Though it prefers a cooler climate, it is able to grow and flower quite well in the tropics.

with many holes, many types of orchids can be grown successfully, and will not require repotting for several years, as the potting media is highly durable and allows decayed organic matter to be flushed out easily.

Similarly, growers in Hawaii have developed their own media comprising lava rock – sometimes with charcoal – to provide an equally well-drained and aerated mix.

Apart from these 'traditional' mixes developed in the early days, many other materials have been added to the list of possible potting ingredients, including organic materials such as coconut husk, tree fern bark, pine bark chips and macadamia nut shells, as well as inorganic materials like coarse gravel chips, expanded clay, rock-wool and even styrofoam.

Coconut husks make a cheap and readily available growing medium for many types of tropical orchids. Here the established roots of *Dendrobium* orchids are growing into the coconut husks and covering them. The orchids have been growing on them for at least three years, as is evident from the extensive root system that has developed as well as the thick layers of mosses and algae, which are a result of years of fertiliser applications. It is time to replace the husks for renewed growth and plant hygiene.

This young three-leaved plant – a *Phalaenopsis* hybrid – was mounted on a slab of tree fern bark and is flowering for the first time. A native of Southeast Asia, this shade-loving orchid, with daily watering on this growing medium, will flower throughout the year.

A combination of styrofoam and coconut husk pieces has the advantage of providing good drainage and an airy substrate, as the coconut husk is water-absorbent and the styrofoam is extremely long-lasting. It makes for a very lightweight potting media.

In the current world of waste recycling, rolled-up newspapers can be used to grow orchids. Use at least 15 sheets of old newspaper and roll them tightly together and fasten firmly with cable ties; soak overnight in water. The orchid can then be attached in the same way as it is to a tree. Hang it up and water daily. The newspaper roll on the left is almost totally covered with a lush flowering *Dendrobium polytrichum,* to the point that the paper can be hardly seen; the one on the right is recently planted.

As most of the organic materials listed will decay in due course (except the tree fern), potting media that comprises a higher proportion of organic material will require repotting more often to ensure the well-being of the plant. That is why the traditional charcoal-and-brick potting media remains popular today – this media only requires changing if the charcoal displays a build-up of fertiliser salts.

In Central America and other parts of the tropics where there are highlands, a greater proportion of organic material can be used in the potting media because it will not break down as fast in the cooler highland temperatures. But as rainfall is still very high in these regions, especially in the cloud forests, the media must still be coarse and well-drained.

The only parts of the tropics where peat moss and sphagnum moss should be incorporated into orchid potting media are the dry desert regions where temperatures are high but rainfall and humidity very low. Perlite and coarse vermiculite are inorganic alternatives for these regions, but because their water retention ability is very high, they should still be used sparingly.

True terrestrial orchids like *Paphiopedilum* and *Spathoglottis* have very different growing media requirements from epiphytic orchids like *Dendrobiums*. Terrestrial orchids require rich organic material in their potting media. A mix of decomposed leaf litter and crumbly loose soil in a ratio of 1:1 is ideal. While this mix will have good water retention properties, it is important to note that the substrate must at the same time be well-drained, because terrestrial orchids do not like soggy growing conditions. Therefore, for orchids grown in the ground, it is best to plant them in raised garden beds.

For terrestrial orchids grown in pots, it may be necessary to add some coarse material like broken lava rock or gravel to improve the drainage properties of the potting media. Do make sure that there are enough holes in the base of the pots to let out the excess water.

When in Rome, do as the Romans do. This aptly describes the use of porous lava rock in Hawaii where its ready availability makes it an ideal potting medium for orchids. Different countries use different potting media depending on what materials are available.

GROWING ORCHIDS ON TREES

For those gardeners fortunate to have some trees in their garden, they will be able to grow epiphytic orchids on a branch or on the bark of the trunk. The advantage of growing orchids on trees is that there is no need to worry about repotting. Epiphytic orchids can be grown on almost all types of trees.

To transfer an orchid from a pot to a tree it is necessary to first carefully remove the plant from the pot and shake out the old potting media without damaging the roots. Position the plant on the tree at least one metre above the ground (this is to prevent the plant being splashed by soil, which is detrimental to the growth of epiphytic orchids).

Tie the stem onto the bark firmly using raffia or thin electrical cable. Use of the modern cable tie is also possible, provided the diameter of the stem is not too large.

A large lowland epiphyte from Vietnam and Indonesia, *Cymbidium bicolour* is best grown on trees, and can grow into a large clump over the years. It has a pendulous inflorescence that hangs down from the plant; the flowers are small and reddish cream.

Brassavola nodosa is a Central American orchid with white flowers and a unique spade-like lip. Here it is growing very well on the trunk of a *Podocarpus rumphii* tree in the tropical lowlands. In the evening, the flowers fill the air with a most enchanting scent.

Cover the roots with some sphagnum moss or coconut husk fibre and then firmly tie those onto the bark with the raffia or cable.

Water the orchid daily. The sphagnum moss or coconut fibre will keep the roots moist enough during this transplanting transition and very soon, within a month or so, new roots will grow out and attach themselves to the tree bark.

A close-up of the *Brassavola nodosa* shows the strong root system and the sturdy attachment of the plant onto the trunk. This orchid grows well on almost any tree and prefers medium to high sunlight – although here it is thriving in fairly shaded conditions.

Although many types of trees can support epiphytic orchids, there are some that are particularly suitable for home gardens, and one of these is the frangipani tree (*Plumeria*). It is great for growing orchids because the trunk and branches are fairly exposed, providing just the right amount of sunlight for most types of epiphytic orchids. As the frangipani tree does not have heavy foliage, it provides good air circulation for the orchids too. Hence, when

Like all epiphytes, *Oncidium* Goldiana is easily mounted on palm trees. Here the plant is firmly secured to the trunk using coconut fibres and nylon string.

This *Ascocenda* Su-Fun Beauty is growing very well on a frangipani tree, as seen from the flowers and extensive root system. Flowers of *Ascocenda* hybrids usually retain the orange colouration and dwarf form of the parent *Ascocentrum*.

orchids are attached to them and watered daily, they will establish quickly and grow well.

The frangipani (*Plumeria*) tree makes an excellent tree host for the attachment of epiphytic orchids. Here over a dozen *Vanda* plants were attached to the tree and they are doing very well, as evidenced by the strong root growth which has covered most of the trunk and branches.

Orchids can also be attached in the same way to dead tree stumps and logs. One drawback, however, is that dead tree materials are susceptible to attack by termites and fungal decay. Therefore if cut tree trunks and branches are used, make sure they are of a dense wood quality so they will last longer.

With its bizarre-looking flowers, *Bulbophyllum grandiflorum* invariably elicits a closer look. As *Bulbophyllums* are epiphytic by nature, they are much happier attached to the bark of a tree or a small branch with a thin layer of sphagnum moss to prevent dehydration. Once they establish themselves, their trailing shoots willl 'run' all over the bark and grow into a clump. When grown correctly in semi-shade, they will bloom with flowers lasting about three weeks.

A native of New Guinea, *Dendrobium atroviolaceum* likes to be mounted on tree trunks or logs. It can also be grown in pots but it is important that the potting media be free-draining. This plant has a short inflorescence and long-lasting flowers.

GROWING ORCHIDS IN HANGING BASKETS

One of the interesting aspects of growing tropical orchids is the ability to grow them hanging in wooden or plastic baskets without any potting media. With the roots flowing out of the bottom of the baskets and the plant hanging in the air, they can make for quite a spectacular sight.

Many people will wonder how it is possible for any plant to grow and produce beautiful flowers from an empty basket. The answer is simple: epiphytic orchids absorb nutrients and water from the rain and store them in their swollen pseudobulbs and fleshy leaves.

Unlike temperate orchids, which are mostly terrestrial, the majority of tropical orchids are epiphytic. The roots of epiphytic orchids can be divided into two types: substrate roots, which adhere to the surrounding media; and aerial roots, which hang in the air. Both types of roots are capable

The beautiful inflorescence of *Dendrochilium cobbianum*, with its multitude of tiny fragrant flowers, is what that makes this genus special. It is an epiphytic orchid and can be grown in hanging pots with a little sphagnum moss incorporated into the potting media around the roots.

Arching out of its coconut-fibre hanging basket is a *Masdevallia* Oriole. The single yellow flower of this hybrid is one of numerous crossings made. The signature flower shape has elongated sepals that stretch into thread-like tips with vibrant colours. For cooler highland regions.

of absorbing nutrients and water from the surrounding environment.

Among the favourite hanging orchids are those from the Vandaceous tribe, which includes *Vanda, Aerides, Ascocentrum* and hybrids such as *Ascocenda* (*Ascocentrum* x *Vanda*). In nature, these epiphytic orchids are found hanging from the bark of trees, with their long aerial roots trailing in the air.

To grow these Vandaceous orchids in baskets, place the base of the orchid in the basket and allow the bare roots to emerge from the slots at the bottom and let them hang naturally in the air. Using thin garden wire, secure the plant to the hanging wires of the basket. It is important that the plant be firmly secured to the basket and its hanger, because if it is loose, the plant will not grow when the basket moves in the wind.

The rambling nature of *Epidendrum quisayanum,* a terrestrial orchid from the higher Ecuadorian cloud forests, makes it suitable for growing in hanging baskets or over embankments. This species is best grown in gardens in tropical highlands above 1,200 metres.

Orchids in hanging baskets should be placed in the shade under a tree or on a balcony exposed to bright but not direct sunlight. They should be watered once or twice a day depending on the dryness of the plant. Although sphagnum moss is generally not recommended for use in potting media in the wet tropical lowlands, it may sometimes be necessary to use a little in hanging baskets because they tend to dry out more quickly than pots on the ground. But use the sphagnum moss very sparingly. Fertiliser can be applied every fortnight.

When the root tips of the hanging roots are bright green and growing, it is a clear sign that the plant is doing well and should be flowering regularly.

NUTRITION OF ORCHIDS

FERTILISERS

Orchids grow very well when they are fed with organic fertilisers. Properly cured manure – from poultry, pigs and other animal sources – is excellent for orchid growth and flowering, because of its high nitrogen and phosphate content. Normally, organic fertilisers, if properly composted and cured, are easy to handle and not at all smelly – but may not be readily available in urban areas.

When well fed with organic fertilisers high in nitrogen and phosphate, *Oncidium* Goldiana grows very well outdoors, its bright yellow flowers lasting over a month. This prolific bloomer is excellent for mass displays in gardens.

As an alternative, there are a number of commercially available organic fertilisers made from substances like blood and bone, fish meal or seaweed. These come in a viscous liquid form and need to be diluted with water. They may smell slightly after applying. There are also organic fertilisers available in dry pellet form in some places, and these are easy to use and usually odourless.

Synthetic (inorganic) fertilisers have no smell and are readily available from nurseries and garden shops – and even hardware stores in many countries. The synthetic fertilisers used in orchid growing are known as complete NPK fertilisers; this means they contain the three major components: nitrogen (N), phosphate (P) and potassium (K). (The letter P is actually the elemental symbol for phosphorus, but it is provided in the form of phosphate in fertilisers.)

Typically fertilisers sold for orchid growing might have an N:P:K ratio of 20:20:20 or 10:10:10, which would be regarded as general-purpose fertilisers. One with a 20:20:20 ratio has double the concentration of a 10:10:10 fertiliser, so would need to be diluted more. For beginners it is recommended that they use fertilisers with an N:P:K ratio no higher than 15:15:15 because many people tend to over-fertilise. Over-fertilised orchids stop growing and become stunted, and in severe cases rot and die.

High nitrogen in a fertiliser results in healthy orchid growth with rich dark green leaves. To stimulate flowering, however, the fertiliser should be switched to something like 15:30:15, as an increase in the phosphate promotes flowering and helps produce healthy fruit capsules for orchid breeding. A relatively high potassium content is still required for the promotion of fruit development and to keep the overall plant healthy.

NPK fertilisers alone, however, are not sufficient to sustain orchid growth over a long period, as there are other elements required by the plant. Therefore most orchid fertilisers also contain micro-elements like calcium, magnesium and sulphur, as well as trace elements like boron, copper, iron, manganese, molybdenum and zinc. Calcium, especially, is needed for stronger and firmer flowers.

All *Vandas* respond well to fortnightly applications of liquid organic fertiliser. This *Vanda* hybrid has the distinctive flower and soft colours of *Vanda* Josephine van Brero, a famous oldie registered in 1952. This sun-loving plant is free-flowering and easy to grow for beginners.

Orchid fertilisers generally come in powder form, to be dissolved in water before application. The powders are usually quite hygroscopic, which means they readily absorb moisture from the air. Therefore once their packets or containers have been opened, they should be kept tightly sealed and stored in a dry place between fertiliser applications.

There are also some synthetic orchid fertilisers available in slow-release form. While suitable for terrestrial orchids, the problem with using them for epiphytic orchids is that the tiny capsules are easily washed out of the pot when watering.

Lastly, do not use the granular forms of fertilisers that are sold in large bags for general garden use. While the composition of these is similar to orchid fertilisers, the individual granules may lodge against the roots of the orchid in the pot and burn them.

In general, most orchid growers are primarily interested in growing healthy plants with beautiful flowers. To do so, a mixture of both organic and inorganic fertilisers produces good results and keeps costs low – giving the best of both worlds.

LIGHT, WATER, VENTILATION, TEMPERATURE

When growing any orchid, it is important to know its individual characteristics and requirements. This is because there is a great diversity of tropical orchids and each has its specific needs. If the right conditions are not provided, it is likely that the orchid will not be able to grow well and will eventually die.

Light

Aside from the selection of growing media, the most important information that growers need to know about their orchids is their light requirements. There are orchids that grow in full-sun (for example *Arachnis* and terete-leaf *Vanda*), half-shade (*Dendrobium* and *Cattleya*), and full-shade (*Phalaenopsis* and *Paphiopedilum*). Only under the correct lighting conditions will orchids be able to photosynthesise and grow well.

In both tropical lowlands and highlands, *Lycaste powellii* will grow and flower. It requires about 70% shade and the potting media must be kept moist. It is seen here growing in a mix of medium-grade pine bark with some charcoal and sphagnum moss added.

Water

Correct watering is an equally important factor in successful orchid growing. Irrespective of the potting media used, a rule of thumb is to water orchids often enough to keep the materials around the roots damp but not soaking wet. It is alright in fact for orchid roots to occasionally dry out for a short periods; most orchids, being epiphytic, are used to the flux of a naturally intermittent watering regime. However, orchid roots should not be allowed to dry out completely for too long, as this will damage them and cause growth to be stunted.

Orchid watering tips

Different potting media will have different water absorption and retention properties. For example, sphagnum moss can absorb and hold lots of water, which can last many days, while brick and charcoal need daily watering. A good rule of thumb is to check the potting media around the base of the orchid to see if it is moist; if it is, there is no need for watering – unless it is a species known to have to be moist all the time.

When the orchid looks and feels dry and needs to be watered, all of the potting media and roots should be thoroughly watered until excess water is dripping out of the pot or basket.

Although watering the flowers will do the plant no harm (after all, orchids growing on trees are watered by the rain), for cultivated plants being hand-watered it is best not to water the flowers as they will last longer if they are kept dry.

A good way of watering small pots of orchids is to dip the pot into a bucket of water up to the base of the plant. This ensures the roots are thoroughly watered but keeps the flowers dry.

And a final point to remember – more orchids are killed by beginners by over-watering than any other cause!

Originating in the cloud forests of Peru and northern Bolivia, *Cochlioda noezliana* is best suited to cooler regions of tropical highlands above 2,000 metres. It's an epiphyte that is best grown in a mix of pine bark and sphagnum moss. It will produce showy flowers for several months.

Ventilation

Most people know that light and water are two important factors in growing orchids. But many don't realise that there is another equally important factor: ventilation. All orchids should be grown in areas where there is good air circulation.

Temperature

Temperature is another factor that must be taken into account when choosing species to grow. Many tropical highland orchids will grow in the lowlands, but they won't flower, and vice-versa. This is because the temperature range won't match the natural growing environment of the orchid. Highland orchid species typically require cool nights – usually below 20°C – to promote flowering. So, in most lowland regions of the tropics, where temperatures at night rarely fall below 22–23°C, they simply will not flower.

Please also see Cultural Needs of Orchids (pages 123–129) for more details on light, water, ventilation and temperature. For the growing requirements specific to the various orchid genera, please see the A–Z listings in Section 3.

HOW TO SELECT GOOD ORCHID PLANTS

There are so many different types of orchids with showy flowers, grown in such various substrates and pots, that it can be difficult for the beginner to know what is a good orchid plant. The first impression of an orchid is usually influenced by the beauty of the flowers. That's fine if the purpose of buying the orchid is just to enjoy the flowers during the period of bloom. But if the purpose is to also grow the orchid with the hope that it will produce more beautiful flowers in the future, then there are four key factors that need to be considered when selecting an orchid plant for purchase.

This healthy *Guarianthe bowringiana* plant, with an inflorescence of rich purple flowers, is a good specimen to buy. Grown in a large pot under near-full sun, it will produce hundreds of flowers in time. (This species was known as *Cattleya bowringiana* up until 2007.)

FACTOR 1: GENETICS OF THE ORCHID

A healthy, lush orchid plant, with beautiful flowers and year-round flowering is a plant that everyone would like to own. Genetics affect (1) the vigour of the orchid's growth and (2) the free-flowering nature of the plant.

Good growth vigour allows the plant to grow faster and shorten the time to flowering. Hence, plants that are growing vigorously should be chosen. They are also easier to look after.

The other genetic trait that is important is the free-flowering trait. Of course, most people like to have orchids that will produce flowers throughout the year. But how can you tell if orchids are free-flowering? The easiest way is to examine the plant and look for the number of old and dried flower stalks. For example, a free-flowering orchid such as a *Vanda* or *Phalaenopsis* should produce an inflorescence spike for every one or two leaves produced. On the other hand, *Dendrobium* orchids will only produce flowers after the sympodial shoot has stopped growing; flowering starts from the apex and then moves downwards. Free-flowering *Dendrobium* orchids are able to produce up to 10 stalks of flowers per sympodial shoot. Orchids that have many leaves but have produced only one or two inflorescence spikes are not considered free-flowering.

A strong triple inflorescence of a fine specimen of *Vanda sanderiana*. Multiple flowering is one of the free-flowering traits to look for when buying new orchid plants. This trait can be easily verified in *Vandas* by checking the leaves, as each leaf is capable of producing an inflorescence.

Hybrid orchids are more free-flowering than species orchids, making them good choices for beginners. The attention-catching flowers of *Dendrobium* Dawn Maree exhibit traits of both parents: the flower form from *Den. formosum*, and the texture and orange lip colour from *Den. cruentum*. As both parents are from northern Thailand, the plant prefers a seasonal climate. They flower on mature pseudobulbs, and these should therefore not be pruned.

FACTOR 2:
QUALITY OF THE PLANT

Even a genetically superior orchid can be compromised by the state of its health, which in turn can be due to a host of pathogens such as viruses, fungi, bacteria and insects. Don't buy orchids, no matter how beautiful the flowers are, if the leaves look chlorotic and dry – that would indicate a possible case of viral infection. Orchid viruses will weaken the plant over time and it will be difficult to maintain.

The most common virus infecting orchids is the Cymbidium Mosaic Virus (CyMV). This virus is cosmopolitan and infects orchids very easily, resulting in a weakened orchid plant with dry-looking leaves with chlorotic lesions. In more severe cases, it leads to flower breaks. CyMV is very common in tropical orchid nurseries, and in many countries some farms have an 80–90% incidence of virus infection in their orchid plants.

If the orchid leaves show signs of yellowing and some are falling off the plant, it is a sure sign of either fungal or bacterial infection. Although it may be possible to control some of these diseases, plants showing such symptoms are normally under dire stress and it is better to stay clear of them.

When an orchid plant is not doing well, root growth will be compromised. Hence, checking the health status of orchid roots before buying is a wise move. A healthy orchid will have prolific roots that are alive with clean white velamen (the spongy covering of the root) and actively growing bright green root-tips. In contrast, dead roots

This *Laeliocattleya* hybrid has produced a lovely bouquet of sweet pastel-pink flowers with bright red lip tips. This semi-dwarf form is less than 20 cm tall, and its flowers should last for around three weeks. The firm texture and rounded flower is typical of *Laeliocattleya* hybrids.

These pot specimens of *Paphiopedilum philippinense* are in good condition, with beautiful flowers and healthy-looking leaves. The species is widely distributed throughout the Philippines in limestone hills 200–300 metres in elevation, and is popular in cultivation too.

can be recognised by the dried, off-coloured velamen and absence of green root-tips – signs that the orchid is doing poorly.

If the orchid inflorescence and buds show deformities, the cause is most probably the tiny sucking insects called thrips. Fortunately, thrips can be controlled with insecticides, and the orchid can be brought back to pristine health.

FACTOR 3:
GROWING ENVIRONMENT

This orchid nursery in the lowland tropics is growing *Phalaenopsis amabilis* hybrids in a coolhouse, using giant fans and the evaporative cooling of water to maintain the temperature between 18°C and 28°C – ideal growing conditions for these plants. The flowers, leaves and roots all look healthy. Pieces of sticky insect paper are hung from the roof to catch thrips and other insects that may find their way into the coolhouse and spoil the flowers or leaves before they are ready for sale.

When buying orchids from a nursery, look at the general state of the growing environment. Is the nursery clean and tidy, or are there heaps of discarded materials (both organic and inorganic) lying around? Are the orchid plants well-spaced – or over-crowded? Always buy plants from clean, tidy, well-organised nurseries. This normally indicates higher hygiene standards and better-quality plants.

Make sure that there are no weeds or mosses growing on the potting media. Weeds are a sure sign of neglect from

the grower. Check also that there is no fungus growing from the potting media – the grey and brown types with soggy texture are detrimental to orchid growth.

Do not buy orchids with roots covered with a layer of fungus, as that would indicate that the plant is not in a hygienic state. Or, if the orchids are covered with a layer of white fungicide, you may want to shop elsewhere too, as that could indicate that the nursery has had problems with fungal infections and the plants may be more prone to diseases.

A nursery on the central plateau of Mexico (elevation 1,500 metres) growing *Phalaenopsis* orchids of very high quality. Note the healthy green sheen of the leaves and the colourful flowers, all free from blemishes. The clean and tidy condition of this nursery indicates that it practises good plant hygiene and therefore plants purchased from nurseries such as these will be healthy and of a good quality. It is essential that beginners start off with orchids that are free from disease to avoid infecting other plants.

FACTOR 4: NUTRIENTS PROVIDED TO THE PLANT

Sometimes it's tempting to buy orchids solely for the beautiful flowers. However, if the plant is not in a healthy state, the flowers will wither faster than normal.

Nutritional deficiencies show up in the leaves and flowers. Yellowish leaves suggest a lack of minerals or the presence of diseases. Sometimes, too much fertiliser leads to leaf and flower 'burn'. Do not buy these plants as they will take many months to recover from the fertiliser shock.

Weak plants that are not growing well should be avoided. Instead, look for orchids with not only beautiful flowers, but signs of good health in the rest of the plant. Healthy plants are green, with a healthy sheen on the leaves, and bright green root-tips. Flowers will stay much longer on plants that are healthy.

AWARD-WINNING ORCHIDS

For most beginners, it is the beauty of the flowers that captivates them, but it may be difficult to be sure if the flower or plant is really good. The easiest way of selecting a good and beautiful orchid with confidence is to acquire those that have participated in orchid shows and won awards.

Most orchid societies around the world use the American Orchid Society (AOS) method of judging; the awards are given in the descending order of First Class Commendation (FCC), Award of Merit (AM) and Highly Commended Certificate (HCC). Each year, orchid societies such as the AOS typically give out 10–20 FCCs, about 100 AMs and also about 100 HCCs. Hence, FCC orchids would be more sought after than AM and HCC orchids; this is likely to be reflected in the price of the plant.

Burrageara Nelly Isler 'Swiss Beauty' (AM/AOS) is an award-winning intergeneric hybrid that combines *Oncidium, Miltoniopsis* and *Vuylstekeara*. It is easy to grow under a wide range of conditions in cool to warm regions, and can produce these beautiful flowers up to twice a year.

An important point to understand about buying award-winning orchids is that they provide only an assurance that the orchid flowers are of superior quality, because experienced judges have done the work of recognising those flowers with the best genetic traits. Other traits, however, such as the free-flowering nature and vigour of plant, are usually not factored into the judging. Thus when buying award-winning orchids, it is still necessary to make a judgement in respect of those other qualities.

When considering particular orchids, it is also useful to do some background reading and, where possible, talk to experienced growers to gather more information. This helps considerably in the decision-making and final selection.

This fine specimen of *Encyclia alata*, with five gorgeous sprays of brownish-green flowers, impressed judges at the 2010 Singapore Orchid Show. It garnered numerous awards and emerged Grand Champion of the show. *Encyclia* is a member of the *Cattleya* alliance.

Winner of an Award of Merit and
an Award of Cultural Merit from the
American Orchid Society, *Brassia*
Rex Sakata is a primary hybrid of *Brs.
verrucosa* x *Brs. Gireoudiana*. *Brassia*
is commonly known as the Spider
Orchid because its long, slender sepals
look like the legs of spiders. This hybrid
likes well-drained growing media that is
slightly moist, moderate temperatures,
high humidity and good air circulation.
The flowers are fragrant.

Though the flowers of this *Vanda sanderiana* are showy and attractive, the plant itself is in a sad state of health due to orchid virus infection. This can be seen from the dry-looking plant, poor root growth and chlorotic looking leaves. Also, the plant has clearly been neglected, with weeds growing from the hanging basket. Try not to buy any orchid, no matter how pretty the flowers may be, if it has been virus-infected and not well looked after, because all these problems will be passed on to you. *Vanda sanderiana* has been used extensively in the breeding of many of the big showy rounded flowers of modern *Vanda* hybrids. Its classic trait is the distinctive brownish-red colouration of the bottom half of the flower, and it is a dominant trait that is passed down to its progeny. Unfortunately, owing to over-collection of this species, it is now highly endangered and almost impossible to find in the wild.

BUYER'S CHECKLIST

In a nutshell, here are the things to note when buying orchids:

- The flowers should be strong and healthy with the inflorescence tip fresh and not deformed or shrivelled.
- The flowers of the inflorescence should be well arranged in a regular pattern with good vibrant colours.
- The plant should be healthy and vigorously growing, with succulent pseudobulbs, healthy green leaves and no sign of diseases.
- For monopodial orchids, the growing tip should be a healthy light green and actively growing.
- For sympodial orchids, look for new shoots from the base of the pseudobulbs.
- The leaves should be fleshy with no signs of spots and discolouration, as these indicate fungal or bacterial diseases.
- The roots should be actively growing, with clean white velamen and green root-tips.
- The orchid plant should be firmly attached to the pot or slab. Avoid plants that are loose in their pots.
- On mature plants there should be many dried stumps of dried flower stalks as evidence of a free-flowering nature.
- The potting media and pot should be clean and not covered with green algae or mosses.
- Check with an experienced grower (a friend, the local orchid society or a professional orchid nursery) if you have a special requirement for a plant.

Striking deep purple spots are the highlight of this *Phalaenopsis* Harlequin Girl flower. Harlequin orchids all have exotic flowers with dark, beetroot-purple spots of varying sizes, the origins of which can be traced to a mutation in *Phalaenopsis* Golden Peoker. This trait has been used widely to create an array of colourful spotted flowers with long-lasting quality. Grown in both the tropics and sub-tropics, Harlequin orchids make popular indoor display plants throughout the world.

BUYING AND TRANSPORTING ORCHIDS

Buying orchids direct from the grower is always the best option, but this may not be practical for everyone. Many orchids are bought from garden shops and florists, and even supermarkets and hardware stores in some countries. However, buying plants from these sources can be problematic unless the turnover of plants at the shop is fast. If it isn't, the orchid plants will be stressed, as the lighting, water and ventilation in a shop setting is not optimal. Instead, it is better to make the effort to seek out good, reputable orchid nurseries – whether from friends or the local orchid society.

When buying from nurseries, ask the nursery staff whether their orchids are new arrivals from another grower or if the orchids are grown and flowered in the nursery. It is much better to buy the latter as it would mean that the orchids have been acclimatised to the nursery growing conditions and are not stressed. Where possible, it is also a good idea to check out two similar nurseries so a comparison of the plants can be made.

Once the orchids have been purchased, bring the plants directly home. Remember to cool the car first before putting the plants into it. Do not leave the plants in the car even for a few minutes as the tropical sun can easily bring the temperature in the enclosed space of a car to over 50°C. The sudden change in the temperature will cause the flowers and buds to shrivel and drop. Be gentle with the plants during transportation, especially the flowers. Avoid over-handling of the plants and flowers during the transportation process.

A pastel-pink and spotted form of a *Cattleya* hybrid with good texture named Monte Elegante. However, the flowers suffer from being cupped in shape and upside-down in orientation – a result of genetics or possibly shipping conditions disrupting the flower orientation.

CARING FOR ORCHIDS

After buying a new orchid, usually the first thoughts that come to mind are: "How do I care for my lovely orchid so that the beautiful flowers stay on the plants longer?" and "How can I grow the plant well so that it will flower again soon?" Here are some tips on caring for orchids that will help to ensure that recently bought orchids will last for a long time.

ENSURING THE FLOWERS ON A NEWLY-BOUGHT ORCHID LAST

Orchids bought from shops or nurseries in big cities will most likely have been grown elsewhere, possibly even in another country. To reach the shop, they will likely have been packed, shipped and then subjected to a transportation process taking many days. During this time, the orchid would have been exposed to many different types of stress, such as lack of light, lack of water and fluctuating temperatures. Therefore, the plant needs to be properly conditioned and specially cared for after purchase. The following are the steps that need to be followed as soon as the orchid is at home.

Light: Determine the type of orchid and its light requirement. Even if the orchid is a full-sun-loving type, do not put it out immediately into the full sun; instead, place it in an area with about 70% sun. This will ensure that the orchid does not get a sudden shock after the period of transportation and the time in the shop or local nursery. If the orchid is exposed to a sudden shock, the flowers may drop and enjoyment of the plant will be marred. The same principle should be applied to half-shade-loving orchids like *Cattleyas*; they should be put in a place where they will get no more than 30% sun. This is equivalent to bright light (without direct sunlight), with about two hours of direct sunlight (morning or late afternoon) at the most. For shade-loving orchids like *Phalaenopsis* or *Paphiopedilum*, they will need to be placed in full shade, which is bright light without any direct sunlight.

It is only after the flowers have shed and the orchid has acclimatised to its new environment that it can be moved to a new location where the full light regime can be given to the sun-loving orchids.

Potting media: Check the absorbency of the potting media in which the new orchid is growing. If it is a traditional charcoal-and-brick mix, it will need daily watering. But if the mix includes sphagnum moss, which is highly water-absorbent, then it may need watering only once every three days. The frequency of watering should be determined by what is required to keep the substrate moist and without it drying out for any length of time.

Ventilation: Remember that all orchids love good ventilation. So, never place an orchid in a tight corner. Instead put it in a location where there is good air movement or gentle wind flow. This will ensure that your orchid thrives. If the air circulation is poor, fungal diseases and insect pests will appear, and the orchid flowers and plant itself will look miserable.

Fertiliser: Fertilisers are not necessary at all for newly bought orchids – the orchid farm would have applied lots of fertiliser to get the orchid to bloom nicely. Just enjoy the flowers until they have shed and only then apply fertiliser.

LONG-TERM CARE OF ORCHIDS IN DIFFERENT LOCALITIES OF THE TROPICS

TROPICAL LOWLANDS

Most of the major cities in the tropics are located in the tropical lowlands. The temperature in these regions fluctuates by no more than 10°C usually – 32–33°C in the day and 23–24°C at night being typical for much of the year. The temperature fluctuation in urban areas will be even narrower, often with a difference of only 6–7°C, due to heat-trapping by the amount of concrete in the city. All orchids love, and actually thrive, when grown in areas with

In its natural habitats in Southeast Asia, *Vanda lamellata var calayana* is found growing on ocean cliffs in full sun – indicating that it is very hardy and thus easy to grow. This small-flowered *Vanda* produces many light-yellow flowers with brown markings.

double-digit temperature fluctuation. However, this is not easily achievable in tropical cities in the lowland wet tropics, which is why it is more difficult to get orchids to thrive in such urban environments.

Nevertheless, it is still possible to grow them well and get them to flower with the right knowledge and some effort. Remember the three important factors of successful orchid growing: the right amount of light, water and ventilation.

If orchids receive too much sunlight, their leaves turn yellowish and show signs of bleaching. This tells you they need to be moved to a shadier location. An alternative solution is to install some shadecloth over the plants. This is a woven or knitted netting made from high-density polyethylene treated with UV-inhibitors. Shadecloth is available under different brand names in different countries (Sarlon is a common one) in grades of 30%, 50%, 70%,

Shadehouses can be easily constructed using galvanised iron pipes or aluminium tubes, and fitting shadecloth over the frame. In some countries they are sold as kits by hardware stores and garden centres. Shadehouses lower the light intensity, allowing shade-loving orchids to be grown if there are no shade trees in the garden. They also protect the plants from large insects such as beetles, grasshoppers and butterflies, and small animals such as birds and mice. (The left-hand shadehouse in the photograph has a large gap over the drainage channel – therefore it will not keep out insects and animals.)

80% and 90%. The grade indicates the amount of shade provided, meaning that 70% shadecloth lets only 30% of the sun through. Shadecloth should be installed at least one metre higher than the top of the orchids to prevent heat-burn transference from the shadecloth as it heats up in the afternoons.

Never water orchids in the heat of the day, especially in the afternoon. This will damage the flowers and increase the likelihood of the plant being affected by diseases. It is best to water early in the morning or in the cool of the evening. Sometimes, when it becomes windy, it is good to water the orchids as the evaporative cooling will lead to a big drop in the surface temperature of the orchid, thus encouraging flowering.

In fact, many orchids only flower when there is a considerable difference in temperature over a period of time. A good example is *Dendrobium crumentatum*, which flowers only if the temperature drops suddenly by at least 9°C with the onset of rain after a hot, dry spell. *Phalaenopsis* orchids similarly require a drop of more than 10°C, with the lower temperature having to stay below 20°C for two consecutive weeks. This low temperature requirement is much more easily achieved in tropical highlands than lowlands.

The terrestrial *Phaius* Red Streak produces a vibrant red colour in the flowers – a delightful addition to this genus's colour spectrum. It is very easy to cultivate and will bloom once or twice a year, brightening up the garden, with flowers lasting about two months.

Warm temperatures, with plenty of sun and well-drained potting media, suit *Vanda* Overseas Union Bank. These conditions are met here by the host tree, which casts only a light shade. This hybrid, named after a now defunct Singapore bank, has a delicate coerulea blue pattern.

Even if they do flower in the lowlands, the result is frequently not as impressive. For example, an orchid such as *Oncidium* Gower Ramsey, with its bright yellow inflorescence, may grow easily in the lowlands and flower throughout the year, but the inflorescence length at most reaches 75 cm. When grown in the highlands, however, between 1,200 to 1,800 metres above sea level, the inflorescence length produced is at least one metre or longer. This is why the highlands are always the favoured place for growing orchids and other flowers in the tropics.

A sun-loving plant, *Epidendrum* Candy Dandy (sometimes labelled as *Epicattleya* Candy Dandy) does well in the lowlands and grows easily. The reed-stemmed plant produces green flowers with a yellow lip and pink column. The flowers are large by *Epidendrum* standards.

Epidendrum Joseph Star is a sun-loving reed-stem terrestrial orchid that will grow into a large clump in the garden. Some growers have reported good results in partial shade and large pots as well.

Although it will grow in the lowlands, *Cymbidium* Golden Elf prefers slightly cooler conditions for flowering. This terrestrial orchid has an upright inflorescence arising from the base of the swollen pseudobulb; the flowers are yellowish green and medium in size.

TROPICAL HIGHLANDS

Highland altitudes ranging from 500 to 2,000 metres are considered ideal for almost all of the tropical orchids, as the right balance of environmental needs for the orchids can be found here. The water from mountain streams is softy acidic and well-aerated – making an excellent watering source for orchids. The constant high humidity with good air movement further allows the orchids to thrive, while the distinct daily temperature difference between day and night of over 9°C promotes flowering.

The erect, single-flowering *Huntleya burtii* is an epiphytic orchid without any pseudobulbs. It requires cool to warm growing conditions and does well from low-elevation highlands up to about 2,000 metres. Its leaves may reach 40 cm long.

Above 2,000 metres, the same principles of orchid growing still apply, but the lower year-round temperatures mean that some species of orchids that are free-flowering in the lowlands won't flower as prolifically at higher altitudes, or may not flower at all. Therefore, selecting species that are suited to *specific* altitudes is key to enjoying orchids in highlands above 2,000 metres. Nurseries growing orchids at those altitudes are the best source of information on species to choose.

An epiphyte from the montane pine forests up to 3,000 metres in Mexico and Guatemala, *Rhynchostele maculata* naturally prefers cool temperatures, but will also grow in warmer highland regions of the tropics, though not in hot lowlands.

This *Miltonidium* hybrid is an attractive, easy-to-grow plant, but it needs cool conditions to flower due to its *Miltonia* ancestry – therefore best for the tropical highlands. The flowers, which rise above the leaves, are yellowish with the trademark purplish-red and white lip.

Miltonia Rene Komoda 'Pacific Clouds' is a lovely orchid with large pansy-white flowers that are slightly fragrant and which last for about a month. It prefers slightly cool to warm conditions with high humidity, so best if grown in tropical highlands at medium elevations.

A fine hybrid for cooler highland regions, *Masdevallia* Joy Edstrom produces impressive red flowers on a long spike. Comparatively, the plant is small, with glossy, vivid green foliage. The plant needs to be keep moist, but the potting media must nevertheless be well-drained.

With both parents from the highlands of the tropical Americas, this *Symphoglossum* x *Cochlioda* hybrid requires cool conditions to flower. It prefers medium light with a very well-drained potting mix. A long inflorescence produces brilliant orange-red flowers.

The award-winning *Vuylstekeara* Fall in Love 'Lovely Lady' (AM/AOS) is an intergeneric hybrid of *Cochlioda, Miltonia* and *Odontoglossum*. It produces stunning lavender flowers of up to 6 cm across that are long-lasting and mildly fragrant. It is best grown in highland regions where the daily temperature is around 20–26°C, in bright indirect light. Allow the potting media to nearly dry out in between waterings, but not completely.

DESERT REGIONS

Most tropical orchid growing is undertaken in the wet tropics, but there are some regions where the climate is very dry all year round and humidity is low. The requirements for growing orchids in these regions are similar to the wet tropics, except that special care must be taken to prevent the orchids from drying out – especially on windy days. If the pseudobulbs of the orchids show wrinkling, this is a clear sign of either lack of watering or insufficient humidity. In this case, installation of a mist sprayer would be advisable to increase the humidity of the air.

In desert gardens, where there may be few shade trees compared to gardens in the wet tropics, serious orchid growers should consider building a shadehouse for their plants. This could be either an enclosed structure or a simple shelter. A good idea is to use 50% shadecloth for part of the roof and 70% for the rest, so that different types of orchids can be grown underneath. Remember to keep the plants a metre away from the shadecloth to avoid burning them.

As already mentioned, in desert regions potting mixes can contain more absorbent materials like sphagnum moss to help retain needed moisture, but even then it may be necessary to water twice a day in the summer months when temperatures may go as high as 40°C or more. When it is very hot, it is advisable to water as early in the day and as late in the day as possible.

In the winter months, however, when temperatures may be much cooler than in the wet tropics – especially at night – watering may have to be scaled back to once every two days, depending on the absorbency of the potting media being used.

HIGH-RISE BUILDINGS

In high-rise residential buildings, the best location for growing orchids is outside on a balcony. There are a number of factors to consider for balcony growing and these include space constraints, the amount and intensity of sunlight, and the prevalence of strong winds – especially the higher the balcony is.

Understanding these constraints, the most practical recommendation that can be made to high-rise residents is to grow smaller orchids. Fortunately, orchid breeders for the past two decades have bred numerous miniature orchids from a wide selection of genera (*Dendrobium, Cattleya, Vanda, Phalaenopsis, Oncidium* and many others) with a myriad of colours. Hence, even with the limited space of, say, one square metre, it is possible to grow two dozen orchids.

Simple stands made from wooden planks supported by bricks are a good way to display the orchids. It would be wise to ensure that the stand is lower than the height of the balcony railings or parapet. This is primarily for safety, to ensure that the pots are not accidently knocked over or blown off the balcony by a strong wind, but also if the pots are below the top of the parapet, they are buffered from winds and will not dry out so quickly.

An alternative way of displaying the orchids is to affix a sheet of galvanised metal mesh to a wall and tie the pots of orchids to the mesh. This is particularly suitable for orchids that are grown on slabs of wood or tree fern.

In the tropics, east- and west-facing balconies each receive half a day of sunlight, while north- and south-facing balconies get full sun for half a year and bright indirect light for the other half. Understanding this lighting pattern and its changes can facilitate the growing of different types of orchids through different 'seasons'.

When selecting orchids to grow, ask the nursery for advice on which smaller types of orchids have been tested and proven for balconies. These would include the mini *Dendrobiums* that are flowering at 20 cm, and which come in many colours, with the mainstays being white, purple and pink. Another genus that is very good for balconies is the *Cattleya* tribe, with small (3cm) to large (10cm) fragrant flowers. The strap-leaf *Oncidium* with a strong yellow

Miniature *Dendrobiums* are less than 20 cm in height, compared to the standard *Dendrobiums,* which are over 70 cm. Both types are easy to grow and very free-flowering. Dr Chia Tet Fatt (left) and Mr Teo Peng Seng of Woon Leng orchid nursery discuss the merits of miniature *Dendrobiums* as a space-saver in high-rise apartments.

An easy-to-grow hybrid ideal for beginners, *Brassocattleya* Yellow Bird takes well to balconies in high-rise buildings with intermediate light and good ventilation. The free-flowering plant has bright yellow flowers which last slightly more than two weeks.

inflorescence is eye-catching and will flower throughout the year.

Because of the breezier conditions on balconies, the plants must be secured properly so that they do not topple over. One way to weigh down pots is to use a denser, heavier growing medium such as broken bricks. Wires can also be used to tie the pots down. Though this may be troublesome, the upside is a breezier environment which allows the orchids to grow better, with less chance of fungal and bacterial diseases. Another advantage of growing orchids on balconies is the relative absence of insect pests. However, the breeze will dry out the pot rather quickly, so it is essential to water the plants daily. Adding of dilute fertiliser can be done at one- or two-weekly intervals.

Avoid growing orchids on balconies that house the outdoor units of air-conditioners, unless a well-ventilated spot can be found away from the hot air exhaust. Orchids will quickly dry out and not survive very long if placed in front of the exhaust. Ceiling fans on the balcony help to keep the air circulating on still days; they should be set to create a gentle breeze rather than a strong wind.

If desired, flowering orchids can be brought indoors for display, but it is advisable to rotate these plants, with each pot spending not more than five days indoors. That way, the orchids will not be too stressed and will contin-ue to flower for almost as long as if they had been left outdoors.

02

GROWING ORCHIDS FOR HOBBYISTS

Mastering the basics of orchid growing is not difficult, and once that has been achieved many people want to learn how to propagate their own plants so that they can build their orchid collections without the expense of buying every plant from a commercial grower.

By propagating your own orchids, you can swap the extra plants you produce with other orchid growers, or even sell them to buy new species or hybrids from commercial growers.

ORCHID PROPAGATION

Orchids that are growing well with beautiful flowers will be much sought after and deserve to be multiplied. A healthy orchid plant can normally be vegetatively propagated after a year or so. A new plant that has been produced by vegetative division will always produce flowers identical to those of the parent plant.

Propagating sympodial orchids such as *Dendrobiums* and *Oncidiums* can be done when there are at least 12 healthy pseudobulbs on the plant. One division can be made for every three pseudobulbs for large sympodial orchids, and for every four pseudobulbs in the case of small ones.

Gently remove the plant from the pot and separate it from the potting media. Use clean, sharp secateurs to cut away any dead roots and then divide the plant by cutting between the pseudobulbs. The divided clusters of pseudobulbs can then be placed into new pots – always using fresh materials for the potting media.

For monopodial orchids, such as *Vandas* and *Arachnis*, propagation is normally done through top cuttings. From the growing tip downwards, count the number of aerial roots, and cut off the top of the plant below the third root. This cutting can then be potted to produce a new plant, while the decapitated plant in the original pot continues to grow. Within a few months the original plant will produce yet a few more plantlets, which can similarly be detached once they have produced three roots each.

For both sympodial and monopodial orchids, once the

cuttings have been made, it is important to soak them in a fungicide solution (e.g. Captan) for a few minutes before potting. This will prevent the cuttings from rotting.

After the cuttings have been potted, careful attention should paid to the watering regime to make sure the cuttings don't dry out. Spraying with a fungicide solution every two weeks will further help ensure their survival. While it is important to fertilise the new plants regularly, don't over-fertilise at this stage. An application of liquid organic fertiliser every two weeks is safest – at least until the plant shows signs of new growth.

One orchid that easy to cultivate and propagate is *Miltassia* Royal Robe. This sympodial orchid can be sub-divided regularly due to its rapid growth. The rich purple flowers are long-lasting, and appear up to twice a year. The genus *Miltassia* is a hybrid of *Miltonia* and *Brassia*, and shows strong hybrid vigour.

Propagation of terrestrial orchids is similar to that of epiphytic orchids, but note that the anatomy of tropical terrestrial orchids can be divided into two forms: those with swollen pseudobulbs, like *Spathoglottis* and *Phaius*, and those that do not have pseudobulbs, like *Paphiopedilum*.

Terrestrial orchids with swollen pseudobulbs can be divided using secateurs once they have formed eight pseudobulbs, so that the new plants will have four pseudobulbs each. They should then be replanted into a well-drained potting mix with lots of organic matter.

For *Paphiopedilum*, commonly known as the Slipper Orchid, it is best to wait until the plant is large and mature before subdividing it. The safest way is to aim for the divisions to have no fewer than four plantlets per division, so that it will not stress the plants as much. Again, a humus-rich and well-drained potting mix is required for the replanting.

Some growers may attempt division of terrestrial orchids with fewer than four pseudobulbs or plantlets, but this is not advisable because the most important rule of orchid propagation is to minimise stress to the plants.

Can I grow orchids from seed?

Yes, seeds can be germinated the primitive way by sprinkling them around the base of adult plants, hoping that a few seeds may be successful and grow into seedlings. However, the more scientific and more effective method is to germinate them using sterile tissue culture techniques in agar nutrient media in flasks or bottles. *See page 150 for pointers on how to buy orchid seedlings.*

REPOTTING ORCHIDS

Dividing orchid plants to produce new plants is one circumstance necessitating repotting. But often an orchid will require repotting simply because it is growing too big for its pot. Most orchids benefit from repotting after about two years of growth – or sooner if the pot is already overcrowded. All potted orchids will require repotting eventually, no matter how well they are growing, and there are several reasons for this.

Firstly, for sympodial orchids that grow horizontally, it is time to repot when the plant has reached the edge of its pot. For monopodial orchids, it is time to repot when the plant has grown too tall and begins to fall over because of the high centre of gravity.

Secondly, potting mixes age and decompose over time; this impedes fresh growth. For those mixes that do not decompose, such as charcoal or bricks, the substrates will over time have absorbed so much fertiliser salts and minerals that the excessive salt present will slow down and even stop the growth of the orchid. Therefore it is important not to re-use any old potting material when repotting – even if it still looks good.

If an orchid plant has become very crowded in its pot, then it would be advisable to divide it

More than two dozen different types of potting media are used for orchid growing. Five of the most common ones are (clockwise from top left) sphagnum moss, charcoal, pumice, broken bricks, and coconut fibre. The ability to grow healthy orchids is dependent on understanding the properties of the media chosen and the needs of the orchids. Highly water-absorbent media such as sphagnum moss should not be watered daily; twice a week should suffice. For low-water-retention media like charcoal or bricks, on the other hand, daily watering is required.

when repotting, rather than just repotting it into a larger pot – unless the intention is to grow the orchid into a large display plant.

In repotting epiphytic orchids, the following procedures should be followed:

1. Prepare all the necessary items for potting before starting. These include the new pots or containers; the new potting materials; wooden stakes for larger plants; cable ties, wire or string to tie the plant to the stakes; plastic tags and a waterproof pen or pencil for labelling. Use pots that are one or two sizes up from the current one. There is no point going for a pot four or five sizes up because the potting media will need changing (because of fertiliser salts building up) even before the plant has outgrown the pot.

2. Gently dislodge the plant from the pot. You may have to break the pot if the plant is overgrown and has roots

stubbornly clinging to the pot. Do not use force to pull the plant off the pot. Using force will cause mechanical stress on the plant, which will retard its growth; it could take months for it to recover.

3. Carefully remove all potting material from the roots, without damaging the live roots. Cut away all dead roots with clean secateurs or a sharp knife. If dividing the plant, don't forget to soak the divided clusters of pseudobulbs (for sympodial orchids) or cuttings (for monopodial orchids) in a fungicide solution for a few minutes before potting.

4. If the pot will be hung up, fit the hanging wires first before putting the plant in. For sympodial orchids, the plant should be placed at the periphery of the pot with the growth point towards the centre of the pot. This will allow the plant to grow the entire width of the pot, thus prolonging the time before it will need repotting again.

(A) This overgrown pot of *Dendrobium* is ready for repotting. When the plant has grown out of the pot to this extent, it is time to find it a new home.

(B) Use secateurs to cut and divide the plants into two halves. Each should have about four pseudobulbs, which will allow it to grow into a separate plant.

(C) After dividing the plant, use clean secateurs to cut away dead roots and remove old potting media from the roots.

(D) Add a tablespoonful of fungicide powder such as Captan to five litres of water, or follow the manufacturer's directions for other fungicides.

5. With the plant in place, slowly fill up the pot with the potting material. If using charcoal and brick, place the bigger pieces at the bottom and the smaller pieces on top. For sympodial orchids, make sure the lateral growth stem is positioned on the surface and not buried under the potting mix. For monopodial orchids, simply place the plant in the centre of the pot and fill up the entire pot space with the potting media.

(E) Soak the cut plants in the fungicide solution for a few minutes. It is important to do this whenever dividing plants to avoid fungal infections.

(F) Place broken bricks at the bottom of the pot and position the cut plant to the side of the pot with the growing point towards the centre of the pot.

(G) Once the plant is properly in position, add a mixture of broken bricks and charcoal to fill up the pot, and make sure that the plant is not loose.

(H) It is best to further secure the plant with a stake and wire so that the plant is immobile. This will help to ensure good growth of new roots.

6. Orchids like to be firmly attached to the substrate or support, so it may be necessary to tie the plant to the pot with string or thin wires in such a way that it is firmly secured and not loose when shaken. For monopodial orchids, it is best to place a wooden stake in the pot and tie the plant securely to it.

7. Water the plant and pot thoroughly after repotting so that any powder and dust is washed away. Orchid roots especially do not like fine dust sticking to them.

A wide variety of materials can be used as orchid mounts, including (clockwise from top left) a tree fern slab, an offcut of styrofoam, a PVC pipe covered with coconut husk fibres, driftwood, a sawn tree branch and a rough wood panel.

G

H

A wooden plank serves admirably as mount for this *Maxillaria* orchid. The creamy-white flowers are borne on short spikes at the base of the swollen pseudobulb. The *Maxillaria* genus includes species that have many different temperature requirements, from warm lowlands to cool highlands.

A healthy clump of *Platystele compacta* newly mounted on a piece of coconut husk. This clustered mini-orchid is free-flowering and produces masses of pretty yellow flowers. The individual spikes continue to add new growths and flowers for years. This species, originating from the Central American highlands at elevations of up to 2,500 metres, requires cool growing conditions to thrive. The shadehouse in which this specimen was growing was open on one side to provide plenty of ventilation for the orchids.

ORCHID NUTRITION AND HYGIENE

The nutritional requirements of orchids were covered in Section 1, but it is worth emphasising for more experienced growers the benefits of using organic fertilisers. Recent studies in the author's laboratory have shown that certain water-soluble carbon compounds are important for orchid growth and they are abundant in organic fertilisers. As such, it is essential to use organic fertilisers, at least as a component of the fertiliser regime.

Organic fertilisers are more 'gentle' than synthetic fertilisers and therefore less likely to burn the plant; they contain a wide range of the micro-nutrients and trace elements that orchids require. Most growers use a combination of synthetic and organic fertilisers, although some hobbyists have gone 100% organic. One advantage of this is that the build-up of fertiliser salts on the potting mix does not happen as quickly as when using synthetic fertilisers.

While organic fertilisers are admittedly more expensive than synthetic fertilisers, the cost can be reduced by supplementing them with simple homemade fertilisers. The water from washed rice or cleaned fish, for instance, makes an excellent fertiliser supplement. Leftover beer and tea may also be diluted tenfold and used to water the plants; they have been shown to promote good growth. These supplements alone won't meet all the nutritional

The dried-up leaf and weeds in this pot should be removed, or they may inhibit the plant's growth. This *Odontoglossum* hybrid, with pink flowers and the characteristic rounded shape and markings, is very popular with hobbyists. However, it requires cool and moist growing conditions to flower, so is only suitable for growing in highland regions.

requirements of orchids, but they can be used to reduce the quantity of commercial organic fertilisers required.

Some growers have experienced good results from applying half-strength organic fertilisers on a weekly basis, rather than a full-strength dose every two weeks. However, it is important to know that orchids only require fertilising when they are actively growing. Some orchids grow continuously while others may have a dormant (resting) period. If the plant is resting, watering with fertiliser is not necessary. If there is any doubt about whether a plant is in a dormant period, it is better to be safe than sorry and use a weaker mix of the fertiliser solution.

What happens during dormancy?

When an orchid plant undergoes dormancy, it will shed its leaves, stop growing and 'go to sleep' or hibernate. The dormancy normally takes place during the dry period, when water is scarce, or the cool period, when there is less sun for photosynthesis. Once the dry season or winter is over, the plant will start growing again and in many cases will flower first before new leaves appear.

Good hygiene is the other crucial factor in growing strong, healthy orchids. Orchid plants need clean environments to grow well and free from disease. For starters, it is important to keep the pot free of dead leaves, green mosses and weeds, as these secrete compounds that may inhibit orchid growth, and they also compete with the orchid for the nutrition from the fertilisers. It is also advisable to remove old orchid leaves from the plant as they are a potential source of disease outbreak. Remove old plant parts such as dried inflorescence stalks and dried pseudobulbs with secateurs. This creates more space for plant growth and flowering. A clean pot will also be less attractive for snails and slugs.

A final point on good orchid hygiene is to ensure that nearby plants and trees are trimmed and sprayed with insecticides and fungicides regularly. This is because surrounding trees, especially palms, harbour many types of fungi and thrips, which could threaten any orchids growing nearby with constant infestations.

The green moss growing in this orchid pot may look attractive, but if it overgrows and becomes too thick, it will smother the roots of the orchid and prevent it from growing well. Hence, remove any mosses right from the start as live mosses are known to secrete substances that inhibit other plants from growing.

A symptom of fertiliser burn is the leaves turning yellow from the stem outwards. The affected leaves fall off in a few days, often accompanied by flower drop. The orchid roots when examined closely will also show drying and shrivelling. Fertiliser burn occurs when too much or too-concentrated fertiliser is applied to the plant. If this happens, flush the plant thoroughly with water, put it in a well-ventilated area, and apply fungicide to the leaves and roots to prevent fungal diseases.

CULTURAL NEEDS OF ORCHIDS

As you progress beyond the hardier and easier-to-grow orchids, it is helpful to bear in mind the key cultural needs of orchids. In Section 1, growing media and nutrition requirements were explained, and the importance of the correct levels of light, watering and ventilation were emphasised. These factors are all part of trying to replicate at home the growing conditions that make orchids thrive in the wild.

Orchids in the wild are found on trees and rocks in places where they can access moisture and organic nutrients. Wild orchids are able to grow by themselves – meaning that their cultural needs have been met. However, in cultivation, the same needs have to be met, otherwise problems like poor growth and diseases will manifest and the plant will die.

So, what are the cultural factors that might be different between orchids growing in the wild and those at home? This could provide some clues to ways in which the growing environment at home might be enhanced.

LIGHT

As mentioned in Section 1, the correct light intensity appropriate for the orchid type is very important for orchid growth. These light requirements range from full sun to full shade, with many tropical orchids requiring varying degrees of shade between these two extremes. Full-sun orchids like semi-terete *Vandas* (for example *Vanda* Josephine van Brero) are easy to satisfy – all they need is an open position in the garden where they receive sun for all of the day. For this reason full-sun-loving orchids, though able to grow on balconies, will not be able to flower abundantly in their full glory. Shade-loving orchids are again easy to satisfy. All that is required is a position where they have bright light, but no direct sun; balconies are ideal for them.

For orchids that require half shade, the correct growing environment can be provided by placing them in a position where they receive either morning sun or afternoon sun, or growing them under 50% shadecloth for all of the day. Morning sun is better than afternoon sun, as the latter is usually associated with higher temperatures, but afternoon sun can be tolerated as long as the direct sun in the middle of the day is avoided.

Some types of orchids may need something between half shade and full shade, or even between full sun and half shade; therefore it may be necessary to move plants around from time to time to find the optimal position for them. Most commercial growers have shadehouses with different sections of the roof made from 30%, 50% and 80% shadecloth, so that they have a range of different growing environments.

Nylon netting is used to shade a *Vanda* growing area, in this case reducing the full-light intensity by 10–20%. These semi-terete *Vandas* do well under such light conditions, especially if their photosynthetic capacity has been impaired by virus infection.

A shadehouse provides the light conditions that *Dendrobium lancifolium var. papuanum* needs to thrive. This terrestrial species is found in wet open grasslands up to 1,900 metres in elevation, and requires full sun to light shade. The flowers last for a week and come in various shades of reddish pink.

In Section 1, it was recommended that beginners not attempt to grow orchids indoors, other than moving plants inside for display for short periods. However, hobbyists who have mastered the growing of orchids outside may wish to try growing some of the shade-loving species indoors.

When growing orchids indoors, note that the light indoors may not be of the right light spectrum and may also not be bright enough. Only full-spectrum light will enable the plants to grow. Full-spectrum light is actually sunlight, and to mimic sunlight, there are special lamps available for growing plants indoors. A cheaper alternative is to mix 40W fluorescent lamps with 20W tungsten incandescent lamps – this combination provides full-spectrum light.

This rare albino *Phalaenopsis* hybrid requires full shade to thrive. Despite looking quite delicate, it is fairly easy to grow. The leaves are typical of this genus in that they are large, waxy and bright green.

WATER

In the wild, orchids are of course watered by the rain, and therefore rainwater is the best source of water for growing orchids. Most tap water, especially in the cities, is heavily chlorinated and this can be detrimental to the growth of orchids. To remove the chlorine in tap water, add a few small crystals of sodium thiosulphate (anti-chlorine) into a 20-litre bucket of water. Alternatively, a chemical-free method is to bubble air from an aquarium pump through the bucket of water for about two hours, and then it will be mostly chlorine-free. Another alternative is to leave the water in a bucket overnight and use it the next day.

By and large, soft water is good for orchids, so in areas where extra-hard water is encountered, growing orchids may be more difficult. Hard water is caused by excess minerals, calcium and bicarbonates. Softening of the water can be achieved using chemicals like ammonia or washing soda (lime) but it is best not to use chemicals if possible. A better way is to let the water sit for a couple of days in a container and let the minerals in the water precipitate. The water can then be used to water the orchids.

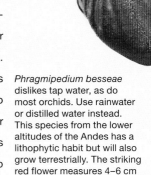

Phragmipedium besseae dislikes tap water, as do most orchids. Use rainwater or distilled water instead. This species from the lower altitudes of the Andes has a lithophytic habit but will also grow terrestrially. The striking red flower measures 4–6 cm across.

Paradoxically, *Vandas* grown in the limestone areas around Ipoh, Malaysia, have produced flowers that show exceptional vase life. So some orchids, at least, are adaptable to hard water. Perhaps the extra calcium in the water gives the flowers an added boost.

HUMIDITY

Tropical orchids love humidity. In most areas of the tropics the relative humidity varies between 70% and 95%,

Miltonia hybrids are well-known for the pansy-like appearance of their flowers. A popular plant best grown in cooler highland regions, it needs to be kept moist at all times and requires high humidity – so good ventilation is important to prevent fungal diseases.

Nanodes medusae, a highly sought-after species from the montane regions of Ecuador, is not easy to cultivate. It requires high humidity, good ventilation and cool temperatures. The soft overhanging leaves in rows end with a bizarre brownish-red terminal flower.

and at those levels all tropical orchids do just fine. Below 70% (as would be typical outdoors in desert regions and indoors in air-conditioned rooms anywhere in the tropics), orchids show discomfort: their pseudobulbs shrivel, and their aerial roots start to dry out, especially the tips. If this happens, the remedy is to spray water on the plant and keep it moistened so as to prevent desiccation. Another way of increasing humidity is to put saucers of water around the orchids to increase the humidity. However, do be careful that the saucers do not become breeding sites for mosquitoes. The best solution for orchids in an air-conditioned room is to rotate the orchids weekly with ones grown outdoors.

VENTILATION

Epiphytic orchids growing naturally on trees experience constant air movement. Hence, good air circulation is essential for most tropical orchids. This cultural requirement cannot be overemphasised because it is the factor most often overlooked. Therefore always grow orchids in places where they can enjoy air movement. This means that corners and dead spaces in the house and garden are unsuitable.

A *Cycnoches* hybrid with a strong upright inflorescence. *Cycnoches* are lowland epiphytes from the tropical Americas and grow well in cultural conditions similar to *Cattleya*. Despite being a tropical genus, *Cycnoches* needs to undergo a 'winter' dormancy through the shedding of leaves. This occurs at the coolest time of the year when watering should be limited to once a month and only in the morning of a sunny day. When new growth starts to develop, regular watering can resume, and flowering will take place in late summer.

My orchid hasn't flowered in two years. How do I get it to bloom?

There are many reasons why an orchid doesn't flower. The first thing to check is whether the orchid is growing well. Are the leaves green and healthy? Are the roots growing with fresh green tips? An unhealthy orchid is not likely to bloom. If it is diagnosed as healthy, then the probable reason would be that the conditions for flower formation are not present. For example, *Phalaenopsis* orchids will not flower when grown in a constant high temperature of over 25°C. To induce *Phalaenopsis* to flower, the night-time temperature has to fall to 15–20°C for a continuous period of two weeks. For other orchids, a dry spell over a month may be needed to induce flowering. The conditions required for flowering are highly dependent on the type of orchid being grown.

ORCHIDS IN THE WILD

One of the pleasures of living in the tropics is the opportunity to visit jungles and see orchids growing in the wild. It may be very tempting to pluck them off the trees and take them home, but there are several reasons to resist this temptation.

Firstly, in most countries it is against the law to take orchids from the wild. Sometimes villagers living in or near the jungle may offer orchids for sale to visitors, but they will be breaking the law too.

Secondly, and more importantly, the removal of orchids from their natural habitats has caused many species to become endangered and some are close to extinction in the wild. Deforestation has caused a dramatic decline in the population of wild orchids in many parts of the tropics, and continued pilfering by orchid traders in more remote regions is only adding to the problem.

This beautiful *Epidendrum syringothyrsus* grows wild in Peru's Machu Picchu National Park. It is a common species in Andean scrub and cloud forests between 2,500 and 3,000 metres. Orchids growing in the wild should never be removed from their natural habitat.

Orchids can only be transported between countries with documentation that shows they have come from farms that have propagated and grown them. The penalty for trading wild orchids is severe in many countries and punishable with hefty fines and jail terms.

Another reason for not removing wild orchids is that these plants are normally not as free-flowering or as beautiful as the hybridised plants produced by commercial orchid growers. Hence it is really not worthwhile growing orchids from the wild. Instead, by allowing them to continue to grow in their natural habitat, the survival of the orchid pollinators that co-evolve with the specific orchid species will be assured, thus letting nature strengthen the fragile tropical ecosystem that is being increasingly damaged by Man.

An extremely rare species, *Paphiopedilum sukhakulii* originated in northeast Thailand, but due to over-collection is now probably extinct in the wild. It was first seen in 1964 in Soligen, West Germany, in an orchid consignment received from Thailand. The handsome plant with tessellated dark- and light-green leaves is about 10 cm long, and the flower, which can grow to 12 cm across, is characterised by lively, spotted petals.

ORCHID DISEASES AND PESTS

Orchids like all plants are susceptible to many diseases and pests. However, the likelihood of their succumbing to diseases and pests can be minimised if their cultural needs are met. When orchid plants are not provided with those needs, they become weak and show symptoms of nutritional deficiency. These weakened plants then become vulnerable to disease and pest attack, which results in a host of secondary symptoms.

The overall symptoms when a plant is not doing well are poor growth, leaves turning yellow, leaf rot, premature shedding of leaves, distorted stem and inflorescence, and weak, discoloured, distorted flowers.

Such symptoms may also be caused by an inherently (genetically) weak plant or poor cultivation techniques, so if the orchid's leaves start to turn yellow and drop, you need to first determine whether it is one of the above, disease infection or pest attack.

A beautiful flower of a *Cattleya* alliance hybrid showing colour break in the petals. It is important to determine if this is caused by viruses or genetics. In this instance, it is more likely the latter as there is no deformity in the petals and the leaves are not showing any signs of chlorosis.

VIRUSES

Orchids infected with viruses are extremely prevalent. Surveys of orchid nurseries in the tropics have shown that in some of them, up to 80–90% of the orchids are infected. As an orchid plant gets older, the chances of it being infected with virus become higher.

Currently, there are more than 10 types of viruses that can infect orchids in the tropics, but only two major viruses are prevalent: Cymbidium Mosaic Virus (CyMV) and

Odontoglossum Ringspot Virus (ORSV). CyMV is responsible for more than 70% of orchid virus infections, while ORSV accounts for about 10%.

Orchids infected by viruses do not die quickly, but are weakened, and as the virus titre (amount) in the orchid gets higher with time, the orchid plant will progressively become weaker, to the point that it is no longer worth keeping.

There are no symptoms when an orchid is newly infected by a virus, but as the virus titre increases, symptoms appear. The leaves become more yellowish, and show discoloured streaks or rings, blackish mottling, or pin-size pitting. In severe infections, leaf necrosis and black patches may be seen throughout the entire leaf.

These *Vanda* plants in a nursery are infected with Cymbidium Mosaic Virus (CyMV), and are showing the classic dehydrated *Vanda* symptom. The high titre (amount) of viruses in the roots are consuming all the nutrients, depriving the roots and impeding them from actively growing. Without active roots, the plants are unable to absorb water, resulting in the dehydrated appearance.

The flowers similarly may show colour breaks and deformities of the floral parts.

Once an orchid has been infected by a virus, there is no cure. That is why orchids are continuously propagated through virus-free meristem cloning and breeding of new hybrids, as the virus is unable to spread through seeds. Orchid breeding thus continues to be the mainstay of staying ahead of the viruses. When orchid plants become virus-infected, it is best to discard them. However, if they are too valuable to be discarded, try to isolate them from healthy plants, to minimise cross-infection.

The chlorotic spots on the leaves of these young *Cattleya* plants are a symptom of viral infection. The yellow-green mottling is due to the uneven distribution of the viruses resulting in an 'island effect' chlorotic symptom. This is most likely caused by the Cymbidium Mosaic Virus (CyMV) – the most prevalent of all the orchid viruses in the tropics.

Both CyMV and ORSV spread through plant sap – contaminated cutting tools being the main means of transmission. One effective way of preventing the spreading of viruses through cutting tools is to sterilise the blades by flaming them with a cigarette lighter. Another way is to soak the cutting tools after every cutting in a 20% chlorine bleach solution for a few minutes.

The best method of avoiding virus-infected plants in the first place is to buy and grow only virus-free plants. They are moreover easier to take care of, being less prone to other diseases.

Black speckling and streaks on the leaves, especially on the older ones, are symptoms of virus infection, which manifest when the plant is weakened. Some of the infected leaves of plants have turned yellow and died prematurely.

BACTERIA

High temperature and humidity create conditions conducive to the outbreak of bacterial disease. Once an outbreak occurs, it can spread very quickly, whether through water-splashing and droplets, or by pests such as snails, slugs, beetles and other chewing or biting insects.

The most obvious symptoms of bacterial infection in orchids are rotting leaves, stems, flowers or roots. As soon as such symptoms are spotted, take action immediately. These rot-causing bacteria multiply very quickly, with the bacteria population doubling every 30 minutes under ideal conditions. Among the most common bacterial infections are the brown or black spots and rots in flowers and leaves caused by *Pseudomonas* and *Erwina* bacteria. Rots caused by *Erwina* emit a distinctive foul smell.

This beautiful *Phalaenopsis* hybrid (*Doritaenopsis* Minho Princess x *Phalaenopsis* New Cinderella x *Doritaenopsis* Sun Prince) is perfect in every sense but marred by the flower spot disease, probably caused by some soft rot bacteria which will become rampant when the weather turns wet and cool.

Though the application of antibiotics can be used to control such diseases, it is not advisable, as it may generate antibiotic resistance in the bacteria population. There are few chemicals that can get rid of bacteria without damaging the plant, but one that can be tried is Thiram, a sulphur fungicide with some antibacterial properties. It is reasonably safe to use, but the powder is highly toxic if inhaled, so it must be handled with care when preparing the solution for spraying.

To minimise bacterial infections, it is prudent to enforce good sanitation, moisture-control (through good ventilation and appropriate watering), and taking fast action as soon as bacterial infection is suspected. As mentioned earlier when discussing orchid hygiene, remember to keep the pots clear of organic debris as these are reservoirs for bacterial diseases.

A typical leaf rot caused by the bacteria *Pseudomonas* on a *Phalaenopsis violacea* plant. It is very important to cut away the leaf at the first sign of the rot, or else it will spread to the crown and the plant may die. In this instance, the plant was sprayed with fungicide (seen from the white powder on the leaves), but fungicide is unfortunately ineffective against this bacterial disease.

FUNGI

The underlying factors for fungal disease outbreak are similar to those for bacterial diseases. Conditions such as high moisture content, humidity, poor ventilation and high temperatures are all conducive to fungal infection.

Though there are many types of fungi capable of infecting orchids, the common ones being the fungal crown rot caused by *Phytophthora*, damping-off disease by *Pythium*, black spot by *Alternaria*, *Helminthosporium* and Anthracnose leaf tip disease by *Gloeosporium*. Orchid flowers can be affected in the form of flower blight by *Botrytis*, and spots by *Curvularia*. Symptoms usually appear during the wet season when it rains frequently and the days are cloudy.

A pair of flowers from a *Brassolaeliocattleya* hybrid whose beauty is seriously marred by a severe fungal rot disease. The dried petals show the blackish fungal spores and this usually happens in plants with poor hygiene. The flowers should have been removed immediately to prevent the rot from spreading and the plants immediately sprayed with a suitable fungicide.

When an orchid plant starts to show signs of wilting, check the roots first, as most likely it will be due to root rot disease caused by *Fusarium*. This disease is very serious because without treatment the fungus will stop water from being conducted up to the leaves, and the plant will shrivel and die within days.

The flowers of this *Dendrobium* hybrid are diseased. Their colour should be a rich, deep purple, but due to the disease, it is 'off' purple, and the petals show a rust-like blight. Diagnosis of orchid diseases is not an easy task, but this is most likely a case of fungal blight.

Unlike bacterial diseases, fungal diseases can be effectively controlled using a range of fungicides. Fungicides are divided into two classes: systemic and non-systemic. Systemic fungicides penetrate the entire plant, travelling effectively through the plant's vascular systems (xylem and phloem); examples include Benomyl and Thiomyl. Non-systemic fungicides, on the other hand, work only on the surfaces they are applied to. Examples include Captan and Thiram, which have already been mentioned, as well as Aliette, Dithane, Physan and Phyton, which are often used by commercial growers. As systemic fungicides are much more expensive than non-systemic ones, it is recommended you use non-systemic fungicides for general preventive measures and treatments. Non-systemic fungicides also are much safer for home gardeners.

A close-up of leaf blight, or Anthracnose disease, shows the wave-like pattern of the fungus's progress down from the tip, and the sporadic curve of the black mass of spores released on the dried leaf. At the boundary of the dried and fresh leaf, note the yellowish band that is caused by toxin from the fungus killing the leaf cells.

These orchid leaves are showing clear evidence of leaf blight, or Anthracnose disease. Caused by the fungal pathogen *Colletotrichum gloeosporioides,* this minor disease occurs when the leaf is damaged or injured by insects, and the fungus penetrates into the leaf cells. The fungus in the infected leaf then grows slowly towards the base of the leaf. It can be easily remedied by cutting off the leaf about one centimetre below the dried tip. This way, the fungus will be removed completely and the plant will return to good health.

Basal rot is caused by fungal pathogens, one of which is *Sclerotium rolfsii*. It attacks the crown and the roots – causing them to turn brown and watery – and progresses very quickly throughout the plant, killing it in a matter of days. Removal of the dead tissues and treatment with fungicides are effective provided the rot has not spread to the rest of the plants in the pots.

This *Phalaenopsis gigantea* is sprouting a keiki (new plantlet) from the inflorescence node. The mother plant, which had been growing very well (judging by the healthy leaves), was damaged by crown rot disease, and thus could no longer grow. As the survival instinct of *Phalaenopsis* is very strong, it resulted in the formation of a keiki. The keiki can be removed when it has developed three roots and potted as a new plant. Continue to look after the mother plant as it will produce more side shoots from the axillary buds on the stem.

This old *Dendrobium* leaf has died and turned brown with symptomatic fungal black spots, possibly by *Cercospora*. The fungus manifests itself as the leaf ages and becomes weak. Proper plant hygiene, such as prompt removal of diseased leaves, will minimise this problem.

The petals of this *Lycaste macrophylla* have been partially eaten – most likely by snails or beetles – spoiling what would have otherwise been an attractive floral display. Pest attacks like this usually happen at night when snails and beetles are active, so checking plants with a flashlight after dark can help to prevent this type of damage.

PESTS

Many types of pests can affect orchids. Some, like the occasional snail, may be considered only a minor nuisance, but others can result in more severe infestations, such as the damage that thrips can cause to flowers. To combat pest attacks, preventive measures are more effective than scrambling for pesticides to deal with infestations.

Top on the list of preventive measures are good plant hygiene and clean surroundings. Normally, if plants are kept trimmed and all debris regularly removed, chances of pest attack will be much reduced. Other measures include fortnightly spraying with nicotine or pyrethrins. These natural pesticides are quite effective and degrade quickly without harming the environment.

However, it is inevitable that some pest infestation will occur in time. Sap-sucking thrips, mites, mealy bugs and scale insects are common; chewing insects like beetles, weevils and grasshoppers are also a nuisance. Ants are often listed as a pest in orchid books, but it is more correct to describe them as a pest-alliance.

Ants

The small black or brown ants that are commonly seen running about amongst orchids are considered a pest-alliance, not true pests, because they do not directly harm the orchids. However, their activities and actions do bring about pest infestations. Ants carry many types of sap-sucking insects such as aphids, mealy bugs and scale insects to the orchids and 'farm' them like cows, milking these insects for the sweet honeydew they secrete. The honeydew secretions in turn encourage sooty mold (a type of fungal pest) to adhere to and grow on the plants, making them very unsightly.

Ants can be controlled with ant baits and traps – generally very effective as deterrents. Household water-based insecticide sprays can also be used, but try not to spray directly onto the plants. In cases of severe ant infestation, where ants have built nests amongst the orchid plants for example, it may be necessary to spray with stronger insecticides such as Malathion.

SUCKING PESTS

Aphids

These small, soft-bodied sucking insects can appear suddenly in large numbers, especially on young and growing inflorescence tips. Aphids come in two colours, black or green, the black ones being slightly larger and having greater sap-sucking ability. The appearance of aphids can be due to the presence of ants, but sometimes adult aphids – which have wings and are capable of flying – may come from surrounding plants such as roses and hibiscus. They may also be carried by the wind from other nearby sources. Aphids are capable of transmitting viral diseases and in large numbers will stunt the growth and development of the inflorescence.

Aphids can be easily controlled by wiping or spraying the plant with diluted dishwashing detergent, or with commercial insecticides in the case of more severe infestations.

Mealy bugs

These white, fluffy, cottony sap-sucking insects are common on many types of plants in the tropics. They may be found on the flower stalks of orchids, on the underside of the leaves, and in between the leaves and pseudobulbs.

Mealy bugs can be controlled in the same way as aphids, or by spraying with a mixture of horticultural white oil and diluted detergent (cooking oil can be used if white oil is not available). A small infestation is often easily controlled by wiping the insects off with a finger dipped in soapy water.

Scale insects

These insects are normally found on the underside of leaves, especially along the veins. They are usually brown and the shape and size of a pinhead. As they have a hard, waxy, waterproof protective shell, it may take several applications of a commercial oil-based insecticide to kill them. If the infestation is not severe, then a mixture of white oil and detergent may serve to suffocate them.

Mites

Two other common pests are the minute half-millimetre red spider mite (hard to see without a magnifying glass) and the even smaller false spider mite. The former is able to spin a web but not the latter. They are both commonly found on the underside of orchid leaves. In a severe infestation, red patches may be seen on the underside of the leaves which when wiped with tissue paper will turn the tissue a reddish colour. The leaves will turn whitish brown under the mites' attack because the mites suck up the cellular sap, killing the plant cells.

As these 'insects' are actually from the spider family, this means they have eight legs instead of the six that true insects have. Normal insecticides will therefore not be effective in killing mites, and it is necessary to use a miticide such as Dicofol (sold under various trade names such as Kelthane and Acarin). Be aware that miticides are more toxic than normal insecticides. A non-toxic alternative for

An attack by thrips has marred the beauty of this red *Mokara* hybrid flower. Thrips are tiny sap-sucking insects that do great damage to the orchid flowers, causing them to become discoloured and deformed. Regular spraying with insecticides is required to keep them at bay.

dealing with mites is to use the white-oil/detergent mix to try and suffocate these small and nasty creatures. However, mites are not as easy to kill with this mix as mealy bugs and scale insects, so spraying every week until the infestation is over will be necessary. This is because the mites are able to lay a large amount of eggs that hatch at intervals of three to seven days.

Thrips

These are equally nasty insects that love to suck the sap of flowers and inflorescence, resulting in failure of bud development, non-opening of flowers, distorted flowers with brown patches and colour breaks. Inflorescence attacked by thrips shows a typical distorted inflorescence development. Although thrips are susceptible to insecticides, control of thrips is difficult as they are capable of flight and they may hide inside the buds and other floral structures and out of reach of the insecticides. Hence, multiple spraying may be needed with severe infestations.

CHEWING AND BORING PESTS

Dried brown spots and tip curl are a typical signature of weevil damage. In many instances, this leads to bacterial and fungal infection – thus compounding the damage to the orchid crown.

Beetles and weevils

These nocturnal insects can be rather destructive as they have voracious appetites, especially the larvae. Beetles eat the soft tissues of orchids, such as the tender shoots and new roots. Weevil attack is normally seen as holes in the plants, as weevils like to bore into the soft tissues to lay eggs, after which the grubs will continue to

eat and enlarge the stem cavity. Insecticides are capable of controlling these insects, but if they are inside the cavities of the plants, they will not be killed. To fully exterminate them, systemic insecticides are needed.

Snails and slugs

These creatures will occasionally crawl over and consume the tender shoots or roots of orchids, resulting in damage that may lead to secondary infection. As they are larger in size, they can be easily picked – at night, as they are nocturnal creatures. However, if there are too many, it would be expedient to apply snail pellets in the evening and scatter them amongst the pots and surroundings to get rid of these pests.

A giant African snail hides next to a young clump of bird's nest fern growing from *Vanda* roots. Snails are a notable pest of orchids, as they eat the tender tips of the roots, shoots and flowers. The bird's nest fern in the picture should also be removed as it will harbour pests and grow quickly, eventually smothering the *Vanda*.

DIY RECIPES FOR DISEASE- AND PEST- CONTROL

There are many do-it-yourself recipes that have been floating around for years. Some work while others don't. The nice thing about DIY recipes is that they are cheap and easy to make and less harmful to both humans and the environment. For this reason, many orchid growers in recent years have turned to DIY recipes. However if infestations are severe, then it is almost always necessary to resort to stronger commercial chemicals. The following are some recipes that have shown consistent results.

Cooking oil and dishwashing detergent mix for insect control

Add 25 ml of clean cooking oil to 25 ml of dishwashing detergent in a small bottle. For best results, use the more expensive dishwashing detergents as they contain ingredients that are less harsh on the hands and therefore also on the orchids. Mix by shaking vigorously into an emulsion. Top up to five litres with water and spray on the plants.

Before using this concoction for the first time, it is recommended that you test the sensitivity of the plant to the mixture. Test-spray on a leaf and monitor for three days. If there are no adverse effects, then the rest of the plant can be sprayed. When spraying remember to wet the plants thoroughly, especially the underside of the leaves. This spray will be effective on many of the small insect pests like mealy bugs, thrips, aphids and mites. As this is an oil-based concoction, spray during the cool of the evening when the sun is setting and the insects are out on the plants.

This concoction is a useful substitute for the white-oil/ detergent mix in countries where horticultural white oil is not readily available.

Cloves, cinnamon, baking soda, cooking oil and detergent mix for fungal control

Grind 5 g of cloves and 5 g of cinnamon, and mix with 20 ml of sodium bicarbonate (baking soda). Add to an emulsified mixture of 25 ml of cooking oil and 25 ml of detergent and shake well. Top up with five litres of water and spray on the plants. Follow the testing procedures as mentioned above for insect control. This formulation can be used for fungal blackspots, blight-causing fungi and *Alternaria* attack. It is also good for small-insect control.

Beer for snail and slugs attack

Pour beer into smooth saucers and place them amongst the orchid pots. Snails and slugs will be attracted by the beer; they will climb into the saucers but will then slide into the liquid and drown. This is a good alternative to snail and slug pellets when there are pets in the house or garden, as the pets may be attracted to some of these pellets.

Vinegar as a weed-killer

Sometimes mosses, ferns and other weeds may be difficult to pull out. A 4% vinegar solution made from homemade vinegar or one from the supermarket is a good weed-killer. Spray directly onto the weeds and they will turn yellow and die within a week. Remember that although orchids like an acidic pH, the vinegar may still be too acidic for them, so make sure the spray does not touch the orchids.

GROWING FROM FLASK SEEDLINGS

Apart from purchasing orchid plants and vegetative propagation, another way for hobbyists to build up their collections at an economical price is to buy orchid seedlings in flasks and grow them on. Flask seedlings can be purchased from local nurseries or by mail order from overseas. Purchasing from specialist growers overseas is one way for many hobbyists to access species that are not readily available locally.

The flasks will contain many small seedlings grown on a nutrient-rich agar medium with sugar. For flasks being purchased locally, check that the flasks with the seedlings are not contaminated with fungi or bacteria. Also, ensure the seedlings look healthy and green with strong roots.

If the seedlings are being purchased from overseas, and it is not possible to check their condition prior to shipment, it is advisable to research the reputation and reliability of the grower through an internet search. Orchid society bulletin boards and social networking sites are all good sources of such information. Check also that the flasks will be provided with the necessary documentation to ensure trouble-free quarantine clearance on arrival.

After receipt, the seedlings will need to be deflasked by gently shaking and pulling the seedlings out together as a clump and washing them thoroughly under water to remove *all* the agar from the roots. Leftover agar on the roots will attract bacteria and encourage fungal growth, which will cause the seedlings to rot and die.

The washed seedlings should then be briefly soaked in a solution of Captan fungicide and transferred to a community pot with the necessary potting media prepared in advance. The same potting media is used as for more mature plants, but a finer grade of the substrate is recommended, i.e. smaller pieces of charcoal or bark.

Community potting involves putting many seedlings in the same pot in order to create a better microclimate for the young plants to establish and grow. The community pot should not be allowed to dry out, and once a week should be watered with a dilute solution of fungicide.

Place the community pot in a bright location but shaded from direct sunlight, and ensure that it is airy with good ventilation. After the third week, a weekly dose of a dilute fertiliser should be added to the watering routine.

This will result in quick establishment and growth of the seedlings and within three months the seedlings can be transplanted into individual pots for further growth.

03

GENERA OF TROPICAL ORCHIDS A–Z

This section lists the most common genera of tropical orchids, to help you identify the key growing requirements for orchids you are interested in growing.

KEY TO GROWING REQUIREMENTS

WARM / INTERMEDIATE / COOL

Orchid growers customarily divide the growing requirements for tropical orchids into the following three temperature categories:

Category	Day	Night
Cool growing	15–22°C	10–13°C
Intermediate	21–28°C	12–17°C
Warm growing	27–32°C	16–22°C

These temperature ranges are not hard and fast. Most orchid books written for growers of tropical orchids in temperate climates list the temperature ranges a few degrees lower, because there the orchids are being grown in greenhouses or indoors. And with climate change pushing temperatures up by a degree or two in some regions of the tropics over the past few decades, even orchids in their natural environment are having to adapt to slightly warmer – and in some places wetter or drier – growing conditions.

Most orchids will tolerate some variations outside of the temperature ranges specified for their category, and this is especially the case for growers in big cities in the equatorial zones of the tropics, where daytime temperatures often peak above 32°C, and night-time temperatures for much of the year rarely drop below 23–24°C.

The main impact that this has on the growth of the orchid is in terms of its ability to flower. As explained in

Section 1, most orchids require a day/night temperature variation of 10°C or more to flower well.

Some genera are suitable for more than one temperature category.

LIGHT / SHADE

The light requirements given in this section cover the *entire* genus, so if this is shown as 50% shade to full sun, it means that some species in that genus like 50% shade whilst others prefer full sun – and other species may have requirements in between. Therefore it is important to enquire about the specific light requirements for a particular species when buying a new plant. (*Please see Cultural Needs of Orchids, pages 123-126, for a detailed explanation of sunlight regimes.*)

SYMBOLS

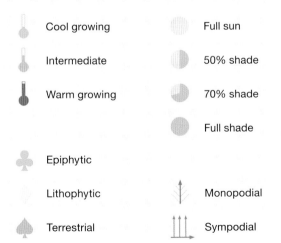

Cool growing   Full sun

Intermediate   50% shade

Warm growing   70% shade

                      Full shade

Epiphytic

Lithophytic   Monopodial

Terrestrial   Sympodial

Ada chlorops is a tiny
tropical highland orchid;
the flower spike does not
grow much longer than the
leaves. Originating from wet
montane forests above 1,000
metres in Nicaragua, Costa
Rica and Panama, it requires
cool growing conditions in
semi-shade.

NATURAL GENERA

ADA

This genus has slightly more than a dozen species and is native to the central and northern parts of South America, mostly in montane forests at around 2000 metres. The inflorescence is an arch and does not grow higher than the leaves. There is a range of flower colours from white to a spectacular orange. These semi-shade plants are not easy to cultivate.

AERANGIS

The members of this genus, which number around 60, come mostly from tropical Africa, Madagascar and Sri Lanka. The flowers are mainly large, whitish with long spurs, and quite pretty, but are not yet commonly found in collections. Mainly epiphytic, it prefers being mounted, requires moderate light and blooms in the cooler season.

AERIDES

A popular genus with about 20 species, it is found in regions from India to the Philippines. Closely related to *Vanda*, the flowers are pretty in a packed inflorescence, with striking lips of light purple. The flowers last a couple of weeks and have a sweet fragrance. This monopodial plant prefers bright, diffused light, and grows well mounted or in open baskets.

AGROSTOPHYLLUM

Found mostly in New Guinea, this genus has around 50 species. It is epiphytic and typically grows at around sea level. *Agrostophyllum* is seldom grown in collections as the flowers are rather small and not particularly pretty, with the inflorescence in a tight ball.

ANACHEILIUM

Anacheilium fragrans is a small orchid with an inflorescence normally of about 4–5 flowers. It grows easily as an epiphyte on wood slabs and in pots. Though the flower is not particularly striking, the fragrance emitted is appealing, commonly described as sweet vanilla.

A widespread genus ranging from Central to South America, *Anacheilium* was formerly classified under *Encyclia*. The plants are medium-sized and easy to grow, with flowers that are pretty and mainly light green with a purplish striped labellum. The flowers can be fragrant like a sweet vanilla and are quite free-flowering throughout the year. It grows well mounted or in pots.

ANGRAECUM

This genus is mainly from tropical Africa, and the flowers are characterised by the long spur that made Charles Darwin predict that the proboscis of the insect pollinator must have the same length as the spur for proper pollination of the flower. The flowers are mostly white.

ANGULOA

This small genus of 10 species comes from South America, principally the highlands of Peru and Colombia. The epiphytic plant flowers in spring and has greenish-white blooms.

ANSELLIA

This genus is widespread in Africa, with distribution ranging across East, West and South Africa. It is found commonly along rivers and in coastal areas, but also in the tree canopy as it is both epiphytic and terrestrial. *Ansellia* plants grow in clumps and can attain a huge size. The inflorescences carry 12–15 flowers that are generally yellow and brown. It is an easy-to-grow orchid.

ARACHNIS

Commonly known as Spider Orchids or Scorpion Orchids, this genus has 13 species and is commonly grown in Asian gardens. It is an epiphytic monopodial and can grow rather quickly, scrambling up a tree with stems several metres long. The flowers produced in long inflorescences are large and stiff, with prominent brown markings.

ARUNDINA

This genus has about 4 known species spanning from India to Sulawesi. The largest, *Arundina graminifolia,* can grow to over 1.5 metres tall; the rest are much smaller. *Arundinas* are terrestrial and grow easily in soil high in organic nutrients, and with lots of sunlight. The light-mauve flowers have a frilly purple lip, much like that of the *Cattleya.*

ASCOCENTRUM

Found in northern Thailand as well as the rest of Southeast Asia, this is a popular genus for collections as the flowers are brightly coloured. The plant is small, compact, *Vanda*-like, and grows well in pots, mounted or even in baskets, in bright, diffused light.

ASCOGLOSSUM

A single species with distribution from the Philippines to Sulawesi, it produces an inflorescence with purple flowers that curl backwards. The plant is a tall epiphyte – reaching 1.5 metres – that grows in full sun.

Commonly known as the Bamboo Orchid, *Arundina graminifolia* is a terrestrial orchid from Southeast Asia. It grows in the ground from sea level up to elevations of 1,800 metres and requires full sun. The plant grows easily into a bush of a metre in height. The photograph is of a cool-loving highland form which produces larger flowers in brighter colours. The flower shape and colour is *Cattleya*-like with the distinctive bright reddish-purple colour and a slight yellow lip. It is a good choice for beginners as it is easy to cultivate.

BRASSAVOLA

This tropical American genus is very popular with orchid collectors as the flowers are whitish, large and attractive, with a sweet fragrance produced in the night. The leaves are cylindrical and dark green. The epiphytic orchid is easy to grow and flowers a few times a year in semi-shade cultivation.

BRASSIA

A highly popular genus, this Central and South American plant is commonly called the Spider Orchid as the flowers of the inflorescence have long tepals that look like spider legs. The flowers are attractive and the plant is easy to grow.

BULBOPHYLLUM

This large genus has over 1,200 species spread over Southeast Asia and the surrounding regions. The epiphytic species are easy to grow and the flowers come in different forms and sizes. In recent years, they have become popular with growers who value the diversity of the inflorescence spectrum.

CALANTHE

This Asiatic genus has a range that extends from tropical Africa and Asia to temperate China and Japan, and has 150 species. The terrestrial plant is normally large in size and produces an inflorescence with many flowers. The unique feature is the fusion of lip to the column and a backward-pointing spur.

CATASETUM

This genus is highly unusual in that the plants are able to produce two types of inflorescence – male or female. In the male form, the flowers have flat lips with spring triggers that shoot out pollinia; in the female, the lips are enclosed in an elongated helmet-like form. These epiphytic plants have thick, fleshy pseudobulbs with flowers of different colours. They are easy to grow and popular with hobbyists.

CATTLEYA

This attractive genus with beautiful flowers and an attractive frilly lip is an evergreen favourite with breeders and hobbyists. Naturally found throughout Central and South America, the epiphytic plants are easy to grow and bloom several times a year.

COCHLIODA

Found in western South America, mainly Ecuador and Peru, *Cochlioda* has ten species. It is normally found growing in the high mountains, thus preferring cool weather. Belonging to the *Oncidium* tribe, the plants grow in clumps like *Oncidiums* and many are small in size. The flowers are usually bright red or orange and are produced as an inflorescent spray.

COELOGYNE

Because of its attractive flowers, fragrance and the ability of some species to produce masses of flowers of up to a few thousand, this tropical Asiatic genus of 300 species is rather popular with hobbyists. Mostly epiphytic, grown under mottled sunlight they are hardy and can flower several times a year.

CORYANTHES

This small genus, numbering around 20 species, comes

from the tropical Americas. The epiphytic plants produce

bizarre-looking flowers with an over-hanging lip that gives

them the name Bucket Orchid. The enlarged lips collect

liquid to trap pollinators. The plants are best grown in

mottled light in wooden baskets, in a well-drained potting

media that can be kept moist.

Cochlioda noezliana produces small but bright red-orange flowers, with a disc of golden yellow on the callus of the lip and a violet-purple column. The flowers are carried on arching, occasionally branching, 30cm-long spikes. It requires shade and cool growing conditions.

CYCNOCHES

Native to Central and South America, the *Cycnoches*

genus is closely related to *Catasetum* and *Mormodes* and

produces spectacular flowers from stout pseudobulbs. The

spike is short and the fragrant flowers are borne on a hang-

ing inflorescence. The foliage is deciduous and the plant

normally needs a winter rest. Cultivation of these plants

varies from easy to difficult depending on the species.

A native of Singapore, *Cymbidium finlaysonii* has a pendulous inflorescence that carries over 30 flowers. In other parts of the world, most *Cymbidiums* are terrestrial, but in the tropics most are epiphytic, and they can grow into large mounds weighing over 10 kg.

CYMBIDIUM

Tropical *Cymbidiums* are mostly epiphytic, with small pendulous inflorescences, whilst temperate types are terrestrial, with large flowers (often used as cut flowers). Both are seasonal in blooming and have tough leathery leaves. Cultivation is easy.

DENDROBIUM

This very popular genus has 1,400 species spread across a large area, from India to the Pacific islands to New Zealand. *Dendrobiums* have very attractive flowers and are widely grown throughout the world. This genus has been heavily hybridised, with about 1,000 hybrids currently registered. They are mostly epiphytic, though some are lithophytic as well. A favourite of many hobbyists.

Native to northern Thailand and surrounding regions, *Dendrobium thyrsiflorum* flowers in spring. Each inflorescence carries 20–40 attractive flowers that are slightly scented. It is best suited to cultivation under semi-shade in highland regions at 1,000–2,000 metres elevation.

The sun-loving *Dendrobium stratiotes* belongs to the 'antelope' *Dendrobiums* and is native to Indonesia. The petals are green and twisted, with an attractive red venation on the lip. Ideal for warm to hot climates, it is easy to grow and flowers throughout the year.

Dendrobium tiongii (known as *Dendrobium bullenianum* until 2010) is a beautiful species from the lower montane forests of the Philippines and Vietnam. The flowers come in attractive clusters of bright orange spread over the long canes. It grows best in moderate light, with light fertiliser and watering.

Dendrobium secundum, a native of Southeast Asia, has pseudobulbs that are 50 cm long. It is a deciduous orchid. The inflorescence is produced from canes that have lost their leaves and is compact with flowers that are small and purple with miniscule yellow lip. A sun-loving plant.

This long cane *Dendrobium* hybrid produces a distinct inflorescence that has a rich brown colour with a fascinating triple helical twist in the petals. *Dendrobiums* with this feature are commonly called 'antelope' or 'horned' *Dendrobiums*. They are very easy to grow in the hot regions of the tropical lowlands and can ramble to over a metre in height.

Dimerandra emarginata is an epiphytic orchid found throughout the tropical Americas in lowland rainforests and at elevations up to 800 metres. The flowers appear in tufts at the end of the shoot and are a pretty pinkish-purple. The flat fan-shape lip is a slightly darker purple and rather attractive. The centre of the flower is highlighted with a white-based lip, making it look dainty. A seed capsule can be seen forming from the first flower. The plant needs semi-shade and high humidity and grows best in regions with a cool winter.

DENDROCHILIUM

Native to Southeast Asia, *Dendro-chilium* plants produce thin pseudo-bulbs with a single long, narrow leaf. The inflorescence is made up of many small flowers that are densely packed and look attractive when grown in a group. They are easy to cultivate.

DIMERANDRA

Widespread from Mexico to Brazil, *Dimerandra* has eight species and these large plants grow as clumps with thin, long leaves. The flowers are beautiful, generally purple, with a fan-shaped lip that is whitish at the base. The plant requires high humidity and grows easily in cultivation.

DISA

An African genus with 160 species, *Disa* produces attractive red flowers that are long-lasting and can be used as cut flowers. However, these terrestrial orchids are not easy to cultivate due to their specific needs and requirements and are quite easily killed by rot diseases.

DRACULA

This genus is a young one, created only in 1978 when it was separated from the larger genus *Masdevallia*; it currently has slightly more than 100 species. The name means 'little dragon' in Latin, referring to the two long spurs of the sepals. These orchids come from the highlands of the Andes and Central America.

ENCYCLIA

A popular genus from the Americas, *Encyclia* gets its name from the characteristic flower structure where the lateral lobe of the lip encircles the column. The plants produce inflorescences with many flowers that are showy and fragrant. It has a wide distribution, from Florida in the north down to Venezuela.

Epidendrum denticulatum is a species widespread in tropical Brazil, growing in both terrestrial and epiphytic settings. The purple inflorescence is a compact raceme borne at the apex of the plant, which can grow into a large bush. It is a sun-loving orchid.

EPIDENDRUM

With over 1000 species, this popular genus spreads over a huge geographic range, from South Carolina to Argentina. As a mega genus, its habitat is very diverse, but as the name implies, the majority of its members are epiphytic. The plants are quite easy to cultivate, and produce the typical umbellate inflorescence with small flowers that have spectacular flat lips. The colour range is wide, but the showy ones typically have bright, orangey-red flowers.

EPIPACTIS

This genus has worldwide distribution, and is generally found in the sub-tropics and temperate regions. However, a few species are found in Thailand and Laos too. They grow on the forest floor where it is moist and wet. The creeping rhizome is fleshy and grows offshoots with leaves and flowers up to 70cm in height.

ERIA

This is a large genus with around 450 species, but it has never been popular with orchid growers and hobbyists – probably because only a few species in the genus have attractive flowers. They are generally large plants with comparatively small flowers. The natural range of this genus spans from India to Australia and the Pacific islands.

EULOPHIA

The 200 species that make up this genus are found across Africa and Southeast Asia. They are characterised by swollen pseudobulbs buried in the soil. The flowers of the Asiatic species are small and dull; not so for the African species. They are easy to cultivate and will flower annually in a very regular manner as they are deciduous and undergo a period of dormancy. These terrestrial orchids are found in the forests, deserts and open wastelands.

GONGORA

This small genus of 25 species grows mainly in tropical Central America. The epiphytic plants produce a fine mat of roots that grow upwards, forming a root ball to catch leaf litter. The pendulous hanging inflorescence has bizarre-looking flowers that hang backwards with their lips pointing up. They are therefore best grown in hanging pots and baskets or mounted on bark.

An easy-to-grow terrestrial orchid for the tropical lowlands, *Grammatophyllum scriptum* is a smaller cousin of the world's largest orchid, *Grammatophyllum speciosum*. The plant does best in semi-shaded conditions and will sometimes produce inflorescences 2m long.

GRAMMATOPHYLLUM

This Asiatic genus is well-known for having the largest orchids; *Grammatophyllum speciosum* can grow to more than a ton in mass! The flowers are in a large inflorescence and are mainly green with brown spots or markings. The whitish roots grow upwards to form a root-ball that catches leaf litter.

GUARIANTHE

Formerly under the *Cattleya* genus, *Guarianthe* became a separate genus in 2003. These plants are native to Central and South America. The flowers are beautiful and showy with an attractive lip, their colour varying from purple to pink or yellow. It grows easily into clumps and flowers regularly. An attractive plant, it thrives in bright indirect light, growing well in pots or mounted.

HOLCOGLOSSUM

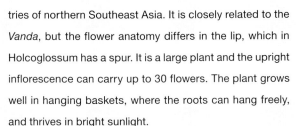

This genus originates from southern China and the Indo-Chinese coun-tries of northern Southeast Asia. It is closely related to the *Vanda*, but the flower anatomy differs in the lip, which in Holcoglossum has a spur. It is a large plant and the upright inflorescence can carry up to 30 flowers. The plant grows well in hanging baskets, where the roots can hang freely, and thrives in bright sunlight.

Holcoglossum sinicum, although closely related to *Vanda*, differs in the flower anatomy and the overall appearance of the plant. The dainty white flowers have red lips and green lower sepals. This monopodial epiphyte prefers warm to cool growing conditions in highland regions.

HUNTLEYA

There are fourteen species of *Huntleya* orchids. They occur naturally in Central and South America at middle montane altitudes as an epiphyte in the forest. The plants do not have pseudobulbs and instead have thick leaves that can grow quite large. The flowers, produced singly, are attractive in both shape and colour.

Ionopsis utricularioides is a miniature species of orchid. The specimen here is a young plant whose inflorescence is still small. With time, it will grow into an impressive plant with a large inflorescence of cascading soft purple flowers. Best grown mounted on a wooden slab.

Laelia purpurata is a handsome orchid with a clean flower and a gorgeous purple lip that has intricate venations in the throat. The plant is considered a giant amongst *Laelia* orchids, able to grow up to 60 cm in height.

IONOPSIS

The distribution of this genus from the Americas is wide, from Florida down to Bolivia. The plants are generally small and epiphytic but produce long inflorescences with soft flowers like snowflakes. The colours vary from white to pink and red. They grow best when mounted or in pots that have a freely drained potting medium.

LAELIA

With large, lovely flowers that boast an attractive tube-like lip, this genus is possibly one of the most prominent in the orchid world. *Laelias* are very easy to cultivate and free-flowering, and have been heavily used in breeding, giving many colourful hybrids under the *Cattleya* alliance. The only constraint is its cool-loving nature, as this genus originates from the highlands of Central and South America.

LYCASTE

A small genus of 35 species, it is found in the highlands of Central and South America and characterised by attractive green egg-shaped pseudobulbs with two to three elliptical leaves that fall off annually. The flower has three large sepals, and the petals are much reduced, forming a 'roof' around the column. Easy to cultivate, it requires cool temperatures with moderate light.

LUDISIA

This genus is found on the forest floors of Southeast Asia in heavy shade. *Ludisia* plants are commonly called Jewel Orchids because of their colourful leaves with an attractive venation. The flowers, on an upright inflorescence, are small and whitish and not terribly attractive; the plant is mainly grown for its leaves – whose colour can vary greatly depending on the light intensity.

MASDEVALLIA

Masdevallia carruthersiana is a dainty epiphytic orchid that comes from the cloud forests of Ecuador, where it grows between 1,500 and 2,000 metres. It will flower freely for several months in cooler highland climates (15–25°C) but the potting mix must be kept moist.

This is a genus with around 300 species, all of which share the same small, elliptical leaves. The flowers all have three elongated sepals with the lower two being much larger in size, but apart from that vary greatly in form and colour. Found growing mainly as epiphytes, they are from the cooler highlands of Central and South America.

Maxillaria tenuifolia is a species from Mexico, where it grows in both hot and cool regions. It is commonly known as the Coconut Orchid in many countries because the fragrance it emits during the day is strongly reminiscent of coconut. It produces one flower at a time, but almost continuously.

MAXILLARIA

A popular genus with 300 species, it comes from the tropical highlands of Central and South America. The flowers are showy and come in many attractive colours and fragrances. They have creeping rhizomes and are best grown mounted on bark or in baskets and pots with good ventilation.

Maxillaria picta is one of the more popular species of the genus originating from Brazil. This orchid is epiphytic and grows inside the forest, but usually on higher branches where they can get enough light but still benefit from the humidity of the forest. The highly fragrant and attractively formed flowers of this species make it a popular orchid in cultivation.

MILTONIA

Native to South America, *Miltonia* is generally found grow-ing in the cooler regions. The plants are sympodial like the *Oncidium* and the flowers are pretty and long-lasting. The most striking feature of the flower is the lip, which is very different from the tepals. This genus is used widely for crossings, which has led to the production of even prettier flowers.

MILTONIOPSIS

A genus with wide distribution from Central to tropical South America. The small- to medium-size orchids have pseudobulbs producing a leaf each. They are cool-loving and the inflorescences produce flowers that are generally white with a broad flat lip that has beautiful red markings. *Miltoniopsis* grow well in diffused light with good ventilation and cooler temperatures.

MORMODES

This genus of about 70 species from Central and South America has swollen pseudobulbs, from the base of which the inflorescence originates. A close relative of the *Catasetum* genus, it can be distinguished by the strong arch of the folded lip. Flowering usually occurs after dormancy when new shoots are forming; the flowers can be quite colourful. Cultivation of these plants can be challenging.

NANODES

The geographical distribution of Nanodes ranges from Central to South America, growing mostly on moss-covered trees in cool conditions with high humidity, good ventilation and clean running water. The plants are easily recognised by their overhanging stems with two short fleshy rows of leaves. The reddish-brown flowers, numbering one to three, are found at the terminal end of the plant. They are unable to withstand drying out, and must hence be kept constantly moist.

ODONTOGLOSSUM

A genus from Central America and the tropical regions of South America, it has about 100 species and is found at higher elevations. The pseudobulbs are compact, with leaf-like bracts at the base. The inflorescence has about 20 flowers, which are showy with spots. They prefer cooler, humid conditions with good ventilation and bright light.

ONCIDIUM

This genus of over 300 species is generally found in Central and South America. The inflorescences are showy with numerous flowers; the lips are generally of a different colour from the tepals. A favourite among orchid growers, it is an easy-to-care-for genus with highly attractive flowers.

PAPHIOPEDILUM

Commonly known as Slipper Orchids for the slipper-like lip, this genus has a range of 70 species from tropical Asia to New Guinea and the Solomon Islands. The two rows of leaves can be plain green or mottled with tessellated patterns that are quite attractive. *Paphiopedilums* are very popular with growers and hobbyists as the flowers are long-lasting and easy to grow. The plants are mainly terrestrial in limestone regions and prefer a shaded environment for optimal growth.

Paphiopedilum insigne has been a popular species in the past as it was used for cut flowers in the winter and also for the breeding of many green decorative hybrids with the distinctive white top fringe. The leaves are about 20 cm long, and the long-lasting flowers 10 cm across.

Native to the mountains of Sumatra, *Paphiopedilum glaucophyllum* is a shade-loving terrestrial orchid that grows in well-drained leaf litter mixed with pumice. The inflorescence carries one flower at a time, thus ensuring flowering over many months.

Paphiopedilum hennisianum is a slipper orchid from the Philippines. This species is easy to grow in an open and free-draining potting mix. The flowers are an attractive green and white, with burgundy coloration, and last a month or more.

Paphiopedilum haynaldianum is a slipper orchid from the Philippines that grows as both a lithophyte and terrestrial on granite and limestone hills from sea level up to 1,400 metres in elevation. The flowers, measuring up to 15 cm across, have greenish-yellow spotted petals.

PARAPHALAENOPSIS

Endemic to the island of Borneo in Southeast Asia, *Paraphalaenopsis* grows epiphytically in lowland forests. It has long, dark-green cylindrical leaves that point downwards, and rambling roots anchoring the plant firmly onto the bark. The short inflorescences carrying 9–12 flowers are greenish-yellow with a dirty brown colouring. This free-flowering plant is easy to cultivate.

PHAIUS

A genus with about 50 large terrestrial species, it has wide distribution from Central Africa to Asia, Australia and the Pacific islands. It is found in forests and grasslands and produces a large inflorescence that has showy flowers with a lip fused to the column. They make excellent garden plants as they are easy to grow.

Phaius tankervilleae, an Asiatic terrestrial orchid occurring in lowlands to lower-level montane forests, has a wide distribution from southern India and across Southeast Asia to northern Australia, where it grows mostly on swampy land. It has several common names including Swamp Orchid and Nun's Orchid. The inflorescence is upright, bearing many brown-and-white flowers with a mauve lip, and can grow to over a metre in height. This plant is easily cultivated and grows in semi-shade. It has become an invasive species in Hawaii.

This tree-fern-mounted *Phalaenopsis violacea* is a variant with a light mauve tinge that is popularly called 'Blue' (there is no true blue colour in orchids). A typical characteristic of this orchid is that on each inflorescence, only one or two flowers are open at a time.

Phalaenopsis lindenii is a mini *Phalaenopsis* native to the Philippines. It comes from the mountains at elevations between 1000 and 2000 metres, so prefers cooler growing conditions. It has attractive mottled leaves and grows well mounted on tree fern slabs or in pots.

PHALAENOPSIS

Commonly known as Moth Orchids, they are mostly found in Southeast Asia, though their distribution extends to India in the west and Australia in the east. There are around 50 species distributed from the lowlands to the highlands and up to montane elevations. A shade-loving plant, it produces an inflorescence with pretty flowers that are long-lasting. It is now a very popular orchid, with numerous hybrids being produced, notably in Taiwan.

PHOLIDOTA

An Asiatic orchid that grows in Southeast Asia and Australia, this genus has around 30 species and is closely related to the *Coelogyne*. The inflorescence is pendulous and the small flowers arranged in a zig-zag pattern. They are not popular with growers as the flowers are generally not considered attractive.

PHRAGMIPEDIUM

Common known as Lady's Slipper, *Phragmipedium* comes from Central and South America. A popular orchid because of its attractive flowers, its main drawback is the short lifespan of the flowers – a mere couple of days.

PLATYSTELE

Native to Central and South America, there are over 90 species in the *Platystele* genus, most of them being miniature epiphytes growing in dense clusters. The flowers are minuscule, measuring one or two millimetres across, and

Phragmipedium chapadense is a terrestrial orchid found in Brazil in open grasslands at elevations of 700–900 metres. Its common name is the Lady's Slipper Orchid, from the prominent slipper-like pouch of the flower. The genus *Phragmipedium* is a slipper orchid from the New World. It produces yellow-green flowers with brown venation, opening one at a time, and up to five flowers in succession. The dark green coriaceous leaves are long – up to 60 cm in length and 3 cm in width. The flowering season in Brazil is at the end of summer.

Psygmorchis pusilla, formerly known as *Oncidium pusillum*, is found in many countries of the tropical Americas on trees and shrubs in grassland and forests. Regarded as a miniature orchid, it is a small epiphyte, with fleshy, flat, fan-like foliage. The axillary raceme produces one to four brightly coloured yellow flowers with brown markings about the size of a thumb nail. Flowering is throughout the year and the plant can be grown on a tree or in a pot. It requires filtered light, high humidity, and regular misting when the weather is hot.

the inflorescence, though long-lasting, is seldom taller than the leaves. These orchids must be kept moist and are therefore found growing in the cool and moist highlands of the tropics.

PSYGMORCHIS

Native to Central and South America, the plants in this genus are very small and do not produce pseudobulbs; the leaves are arranged in two rows in a fan shape. The yellow flower is pretty with brown spots and markings, typical of an *Oncidium* flower. Because of its small size, the plant is shade-loving and requires constant misting and good ventilation.

PTEROSTYLIS

A terrestrial orchid with around 100 species, it is mainly temperate, although a few species are found in Papua New Guinea. The characteristic feature of the flower is the hood-like top sepal, hence it is commonly called Greenhood. The plant is deciduous.

RENANTHERA

An Asiatic orchid naturally found in India, China, Southeast Asia and New Guinea. It is a tall monopodial with yellow-and-red flowers borne on a large inflorescence. It is sun-loving and easy to grow, and will flower a couple of times a year. A popular genus, it is commercially grown as cut flowers and pot plants for its fiery-red flowers.

RESTREPIA

This genus is closely related to the *Pleurothallis*, with around 50 species. They are small plants lacking pseudobulbs. The plant is epiphytic and flowers are borne from the base of the leaves; they have fused lateral sepals and can be rather colourful. Under the right conditions, they flower the whole year round. It is found in the Andes highlands, thriving in the cool, moist climate.

RESTREPIELLA

This genus has only one known species, *Restrepiella ophiocephala,* which is distributed from Mexico to Costa Rica. It grows along the sides of rivers, up to the mid-highlands, and is morphologically similar to *Restrepia.*

RHYNCHOLAELIA

Found throughout Central America, this genus is closely related to the *Brassavola* genus. It has two species, whose leaves are thick and hard like the *Cattleya*. The flower is produced singly and is large and greenish-white, with a showy lip. *Rhyncholaelia* is easy to cultivate either in pots or mounted on a wood slab, and will bloom quite readily in the warmer regions of the tropics.

RHYNCHOSTELE

Originating from the cool highlands of Central to tropical South America, *Rhynchostele* is an epiphyte with a short creeping rhizome that produces a thick, fleshy pseudobulb with two or three bright-green leaves. The inflorescence is erect with pendant showy flowers that have distinct markings. The plants can be potted or mounted, but require a well-drained substrate for good growth.

RHYNCHOSTYLIS

Commonly known as the Foxtail Orchid because of its bushy red-and-purple inflorescence, this popular genus has four known species, all found in Southeast Asia. The hardy plant is rather compact, with spectacular hanging inflorescence.

RODRIGUEZIA

An epiphytic genus found in Central and tropical South America in both the warm lowlands and the cool mountains, *Rodriguezia* plants are hardy and can be grown in any well-drained potting media or mounted. The flowers are small

Rodriguezia lanceolata is a pretty semi-miniature orchid that is epiphytic and looks best mounted, although it will do just fine in a small pot. The flowers are a bright rosy-pink colour and the plant is free-flowering. A unique feature of the species is that all the flowers on the inflorescence face upwards with the lateral sepals forming a spur. It is easy to grow in tropical lowlands provided the potting media is well-drained and there is good air circulation. It requires high humidity and partial shade.

but colourful in an arching inflorescence. The prominent feature of the flower is the spur producing nectar that is used to attract the pollinator.

SPATHOGLOTTIS

Spathoglottis alba is an albino form of the original purple flower. *Spathoglottis* is a fully terrestrial orchid that needs well-drained soil high in organic content. It is extremely free-flowering all year round. This orchid is a native of Southeast Asia, where it has different colour variants.

This Asiatic genus has 55 species which are distributed from the foothills of the Himalayas across Asia to the Pacific islands. The sun-loving plant is terrestrial and has palm-like pleated leaves with a showy inflorescence. They are easy to grow and make good garden plants, flowering throughout the year in the sun.

SPECKLINIA

This genus, carved out from the bigger genus of *Pleurothallis,* has a wide distribution, from the United States to South America in the montane ranges. Generally, *Specklinia* are small plants with an inflorescence of minuscule flowers and reduced pseudobulbs.

STANHOPEA

This genus originates in South America, from Costa Rica to the Andes. The flower is bizarre and eye-catching as the inflorescence hangs down beneath the plant with large, spotted flowers. *Stanhopea* is best grown in baskets in locations where there is room for the inflorescence to grow downwards.

STELIS

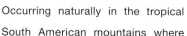

A large genus of 250 species from Central America. The flowers are small and not considered very attractive. It is therefore not an interesting genus for most hobbyists – even though they are easy to cultivate.

Specklinia aristata is a small-growing epiphytic orchid from the rainforests and cloud forests of countries around the Caribbean. It grows into a tight little rounded bush. The flowers are quite inconspicuous, so it is more of a collector's item these days and rarely found in the wild.

SYMPHOGLOSSUM

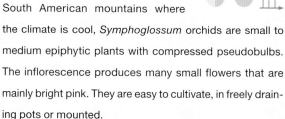

Occurring naturally in the tropical South American mountains where the climate is cool, *Symphoglossum* orchids are small to medium epiphytic plants with compressed pseudobulbs. The inflorescence produces many small flowers that are mainly bright pink. They are easy to cultivate, in freely draining pots or mounted.

Telipogon griesbeckii's yellow flowers have a distinctive reddish venation radiating out from the centre. This orchid is found in high montane cloud forests growing on tree twigs, as it is a fairly small plant. It is difficult to grow as it requires shade and cool to intermediate temperatures. In cultivation the plant prefers mounting as it requires high air circulation (to prevent fungal rot), as well as constant misting.

TELIPOGON

This genus is widespread from the Caribbean islands to the mountains of tropical South America. *Telipogon* is a cool-loving orchid, small in size, but whose flower is spectacular, with strong markings in the petals, and can sometimes be the same size as the whole plant. The lip is petal-like, giving it a distinctive appearance. The plant is not easy to cultivate as it prefers cool weather in the shade with strong ventilation. It is best grown mounted or in a well-drained potting mix.

THRIXSPERMUM

A large monopodial orchid found across Asia, ranging from India and Sri Lanka to the Pacific islands. The species number well over 100, but the flowers do not last – at most a day or so. Hence, it is not a popular genus among orchid growers.

TRIAS

This miniature genus from Laos, Myanmar and Thailand has curious-looking pseudobulbs and leaves. The flowers are colourful and triangular, with a nice lip. They are epiphytic and relatively easy to grow.

TRICHOCENTRUM

A South American genus with 20 species, these plants produce beautiful flowers that are spotted with red dots. It is epiphytic and grows easily in cultivation.

TRICHOGLOTTIS

There are 60 species in this Asiatic genus found in regions from Sri Lanka to Indonesia and Australia. The long climbing stems with short, narrow leaves bear a short inflorescence of one to three small flowers. They are easy to grow, and some showier species can produce many colourful flowers.

Trichoglottis brachiata is a lovely, fragrant orchid with striking maroon tepals and a whitish lip. It likes warmth and humidity, and blooms singularly – or sometimes in pairs – from the stem.

Trichoglottis latisepala is a monopodial epiphyte with long climbing and hanging stems. It bears small clusters of bright pink flowers on a short axillary inflorescence. Plants can be staked together for formal mass display. Grows well in both hot and warm lowland regions.

Vanda brunnea is a typical hard-stem *Vanda* with fragrant flowers that are shiny-brown with a white centre. Although it will flower in the lowlands, it performs best when grown in the cooler highlands.

VANDA

One of the most popular genera, this orchid is found across Asia, from India to Australia. A monopodial orchid, it produces many flowers in one inflorescence and some can be quite large and showy. They are generally warm-loving and can be grown easily in hanging pots and baskets. Many of *Vanda*'s 50 species produce fragrant flowers; the genus has thus been extensively hybridised.

Fragrant orchids

Everyone loves orchids that have a nice fragrance, and with around 15–20% of all orchids fragrant to some extent, there are plenty to choose from. In fact, some hobbyists specialise in growing just fragrant orchids.

Generally speaking, species orchids are more likely to be scented than hybrid orchids. This is because while growers were hybridising orchids, they were focusing on making the flowers prettier and did not pay too much attention to the scent. However, in the wild, many orchids make use of scent to lure their pollinators to the flowers.

When buying orchids for fragrance, remember that they may not be fragrant during the day. Some are fragrant only at night, while others are most strongly scented early in the morning or in the evening. Some may be fragrant throughout the day but other factors like the maturity of the flower or the humidity in the air may come into play.

Phalaenopsis bellina is an example of an orchid that has a strong fragrance through most of the day – often described as resembling sweet violet. The flowers of other genera like *Aerides*, as well as some small strap-leaf *Vandas*, are also fragrant during the day and have been described as being like sweet jasmine or vanilla. Others like *Brassavola nodusa* have flowers that are fragrant at night.

Not all scented orchids have a nice fragrance. The flowers of some *Bulbophyllum* smell like the carcass of a dead animal, as their pollinators are small flies!

VANILLA

This genus has 100 species and is distributed in the tropics around the world. The plants are creepers with vine-like stems. They grow quite quickly, able to scramble up most objects to reach the sunny spots. The flowers are borne on short inflorescences and are green in colour. They are generally easy to cultivate. The most famous member of the genus is *Vanilla planifolia,* from whose fruit we get vanilla essence.

ZYGOPETALUM

A genus from the mountains of tropical South America, *Zygopetalum* plants are mainly epiphytic with robust growth. The flowers are distinctive, with green tepals and an attractive lip in a different colour, normally pink or purple. The inflorescence is long and erect, carrying many long-lasting medium-sized flowers, which are popular as cut flowers. They can be grown in pots or mounted.

MAN-MADE GENERA

Man's obsession with orchids has resulted in over 100,000 manmade hybrids being registered with the Royal Horticultural Society in London. Together with these hybrids, Man has also created numerous new genera, many of which are *multigeneric* crosses, which can be quite confusing to the beginner. Due to the complexity of multigeneric crossing, it is difficult to summarise

Brassolaeliocattleya Arom Gold 'Kultana' is a showy orchid that produces large yellow flowers with magenta frilled lips. This hybrid is popular with hobbyists as it is easy to grow. It needs bright indirect light and will flower a couple of times a year when looked after.

Brassolaeliocattleya Lucky Strike produces large, attractive flowers in rich purple, with frilly lips and a distinctive white column. The outstanding feature of this unifoliate orchid is the size of its flowers in relation to the plant. It flowers regularly with each new growth, and the flowers last about two weeks.

the characteristics and growing conditions of man-made genera in the same manner as natural genera. Generally speaking, though, orchids within the man-made genera are easier to grow than many natural species.

The following are of some of the most well-known and commonly grown man-made genera in tropical countries:

Adaglossum (*Ada* x *Odontoglossum*)

Arachnostylis (*Arachnis* x *Rhynchostylis*)

Aranda (*Arachnis* x *Vanda*)

Ascocenda (*Vanda* x *Ascocentrum*)

Bokchoonara (*Arachnis* x *Ascocentrum* x
    Phalaenopsis x *Vanda*)

Brassocattleya (*Brassavola* x *Cattleya*)

Brassolaeliocattleya (*Brassavola* x *Laelia* x *Cattleya*)

Cattleytonia (*Cattleya* x *Broughtonia*)

Colmanara (*Miltonia* x *Odontoglossum* x *Oncidium*)

Doritaenopsis (*Doritis* x *Phalaenopsis*)

Epicattleya (*Epidendrum* x *Cattleya*) or
    (*Encyclia* x *Cattleya*)

Iwanagara (*Brassavola* x *Cattleya* x *Diacrium* x *Laelia*)

Laeliocattleya (*Laelia* x *Cattleya*)

Laycockara (*Arachnis* × *Phalaenopsis* × *Vandopsis*)

Miltassia (*Miltonia* x *Brassia*)

Mokara (*Arachnis* x *Ascocentrum* x *Vanda*)

Odontonia (*Odontoglossum* x *Miltonia*)

Potinara (*Brassavola* x *Laelia* x *Cattleya* x *Sophronitis*)

Renantanda (*Renanthera* x *Vanda*)

Sophrocattleya (*Sophronitis* x *Cattleya*)

Sophrolaeliocattleya (*Sophronitis* x *Laelia* x *Cattleya*)

Vuylstekeara (*Cochlioda* x *Miltonia* x *Odontoglossum*)

GLOSSARY

Aerial roots	Roots that are growing in the air.
Agar	An edible gelling agent made from seaweed.
Alleles	Different forms of a gene.
Anak	A vegetative offshoot or plantlet from the parent plant.
Anther	The male part of the flower that bears the pollinia.
Anther cap	The protective cover beneath which the pollinia lies.
Apex	The topmost portion of the shoot.
Apical meristem	The group of actively dividing cells found in the apex of the shoot.
Apical bud	The entire tip of the apical shoot.
Axillary bud	The lateral bud at the nodes of the stem.
Bacteria	A microscopic unicellular organism, which may cause disease.
Basal	The bottom end of the plant.
Bifoliate	An orchid producing pseudobulbs with two leaves.
Cane *Dendrobium*	An 'antelope' or 'horn' form of *Dendrobium* with long, hard pseudobulbs.
Capsule	The seed pod of an orchid, normally containing many thousands of minute seeds.
Chlorotic	Destruction of chlorophyll, normally by diseases or nutrient deficiency, resulting in yellowish coloration of the leaf and/or stem.
Clone	Genetically identical plants obtained from different techniques of vegetative propagation.
Colour break	Abnormal colour streaks on orchid flowers caused mostly by virus infection or sometimes genetic defects.
Column	The fused structure of the orchids' male and female parts, bearing the anther and stigma.
Compot	A community pot where many seedlings are planted together.
Cross	The progeny resulting from the pollination of a flower with pollen from another plant.
Cross-pollination	The act of pollinating a flower with pollen from another plant.

Crown	The top central leafy portion of the plant where new leaves are formed.
Cuticle	The protective waxy layer on the surface of the leaf or flower.
Cultivar	A specific plant of a cultivated variety.
Deciduous	Refers to plants that undergo the periodic shedding of leaves at the end of each growing season or upon maturity.
Determinate	Refers to the growth of sympodial orchids where the lateral pseudobulbs cease growing upon maturity.
Diploid	Having the normal two sets of chromosomes.
Dormancy	Resting period where there is no growth.
Embryo	The fertilised zygote that has developed into a 'miniaturised' plant found in a seed.
Epiphytic	A term for plants that grow by attaching themselves to trees instead of the ground and are not parasitic.
Flower spike	The young and developing inflorescence.
Gamete	A mature reproductive cell that unites with another cell to form a new organism.
Genera	The plural of genus.
Genome	The entirety of the organism's hereditary genetic information stored as DNA.
Genus	A classification unit where a group of plants with similar characteristics are grouped together. It is one level higher than species.
Grex	A group of progeny of a specific cross.
Haploid	Having one set of chromosome – normally found in gametes such as pollen and ovules.
Humus	The decayed remains of organic materials rich in nutrients for plant growth.
Hybrid	Progeny from the union of two different species, or of a species and hybrid, or of two hybrids.
Hybridisation	The process of creating a hybrid.
Inflorescence	The portion of the orchid that bears the flowers.
Keiki	A plantlet that develops from a pseudobulb or a flower stalk of the parent plant.

Labellum	The third petal of an orchid flower that has been modified into a lip.
Lateral	Refers to bud or growth from the side as opposed to the tips.
Lip	The common term for the orchid labellum.
Lithophytic	Refers to plants growing on the surfaces of rocks.
Meristem	The active dividing cells found in the tip of the bud, root and stem.
Micropropagation	Multiplication of new orchid plants through tissue culture techniques.
Miticide	A chemical concoction specially formulated to kill mites.
Monocotyledons	One of the two main groups of flowering plants, to which orchids belong.
Monopodial	A unidirectional single stem upward growth.
Multigeneric	A hybrid with parentage of three of more genera.
Necrotic	Having patches of dead and/or rotting tissues.
NPK	The three major components of general purpose fertiliser: Nitrogen (N), Phosphorus (P) and Potassium (K).
Ovule	The female gamete in the ovary.
Peloric	A bizarre manifestation of the orchid flower, where the two petals exhibit lip-like structure and colour.
Pendulous	Downward-hanging, usually soft and swaying in the wind.
Petal	The part of the flower that is coloured and most showy.
Photosynthesis	The process where the chlorophyll in the green leaf or stem harness the light and in the presence of carbon dioxide manufacture glucose.
Plantlet	A new and small 'baby' plant produced vegetatively.
Pod	The common term for the orchid fruit.
Pollen	The male gamete of flowering plants.
Pollinia	The fused waxy yellow pollen masses of orchids.
Polyploidy	Having more than two sets of chromosomes.
Primary hybrid	A progeny with two species as parents.
Progeny	Offspring or descendant.

Pseudobulb	A thick, swollen stem arising from the rhizome of a sympodial orchid.
Rhizome	A horizontal creeping stem, which in a sympodial orchid is capable of producing roots, pseudobulbs and even flowers.
Sepal	The outermost whorl of the flower and which in orchids is normally modified into a petal-like form.
Species	The basic unit in the classification system where the organisms are capable of breeding naturally.
Sphagnum moss	A dried moss with high water-absorption capability harvested from swampy bogs in temperate countries.
Spur	The elongated extension of the base of the lip which contains nectar.
Stigma	The sticky female organ that is found beneath the column where pollen is deposited during pollination.
Substrate	The base or material on which the plant grows.
Sympodial	An orchid growth form where the stem grows along the substrate and produces a series of pseudobulbs as it grows.
Tepal	A loose term for the collection of sepals and petals.
Terete	Describes orchid leaves that are cylindrical in shape.
Terrestrial	Growing on the ground (i.e. in soil).
Tetraploid	Having four sets of chromosomes.
Tree fern	A large, tree-like fern whose stem is cut and harvested for growing orchid plants.
Tribe	A related group of genera capable of crossing, e.g., 'the Vandaceous tribe'.
Trigeneric	A progeny with a three-genera parentage.
Triploid	Having three sets of chromosomes.
Unifoliate	A pseudobulb producing a single leaf.
Variety	A variant of a species.
Velamen	The whitish outermost layer of the orchid root that is water-absorbent.
Virus	An infectious disease-causing particle composed of nucleic acid (DNA and/or RNA) with a protein coat.
Zygote	The cell produced by the union of two gametes.

ACKNOWLEDGEMENTS

We would like to acknowledge the cooperation of the following botanic gardens, nurseries, institutions, organisations and private gardens around the world that helped to facilitate the photography for this book:

Australia	Flecker Botanic Gardens, Cairns
	George Brown Botanic Gardens, Darwin
Costa Rica	Jardín Botánico Lankester, Cartago
	Jardín de Orquídeas de Monteverde
	Jardín Botánico de Orquídeas, La Garita
	Orchimex, Puntarenas
	Alegria Residencial, Alajuela
Cuba	Jardín de Orquídeas, Soroa
Ecuador	Jardín de Orquídeas, Mindo
	Jardín Botánico, Quito
Hawaii	World Botanical Gardens, Hakalau
	Nani Mau Gardens, Hilo
	Foster Botanical Garden, Honolulu
	Tropical Gardens of Maui, Kahului
	Hawaii Tropical Botanical Garden, Onomea Bay
	Akatsuka Orchid Gardens, Volcano
India	Abraham's Spice Garden, Kumily, Kerala
Indonesia	Bogor Botanic Gardens
	Cibodas Botanic Gardens, Cipanas, Cianjur
	Taman Anggrek, Jakarta
Malaysia	Kuala Lumpur Orchid Garden
Mexico	Tahí Flores Exóticas, Yautepec, Morelos

Panama	Finca Dracula, Guadalupe, Cerro Punta
Peru	Machu Picchu National Park
Philippines	Linda's Orchids, Timberland Heights, San Mateo
	Philippine Orchid Society, Quezon City
	Puentespina Orchids, Davao
Singapore	Singapore Botanic Gardens
	Orchid Society of Southeast Asia
	Song Orchids, Choa Chu Kang
	Woon Leng Orchid Nursery, Choa Chu Kang
	Steven Neo and Evelyn Tay, Mandai
Thailand	Nong Nooch Tropical Garden, Chonburi
Vietnam	Tran Tuan Anh Orchid Nursery, Hanoi

In addition we express our thanks to the following individuals who helped in the identification of some of the species and hybrids featured in this book:

- Elaine Acosta of Finca Dracula, Cerro Punta, Panama
- Puah Gik Song of Song Orchids, Singapore
- Teo Woon Cheng and Teo Peng Seng of Woon Leng Orchid Nursery, Singapore
- Lee Nam Fook, Low Siew Ping and Khairi Mohd, Malaysia. The *Catasetum* Memoria Kampar Yip x *Catasetum* Memoria Hon San on the front cover is one of Mr Lee's hybrids.

Finally, our thanks also go to George Hawkins and Luis Barrantes (Costa Rica), Parni Hadi (Indonesia) and Gaston Melo (Mexico), and Vincent Tan and Gan Cheong Weei (Singapore) for their valued help in arranging visits to orchid gardens and other locations for photography.

The national flower of Belize, where it is known as the Black Orchid, *Prosthechea cochleata* is easy to grow and flowers throughout the year. The flower is not really black – the labellum is a dark purple, and forms a hood over the column, contrasting dramatically with the light-green tepals.